Population Education

DPH Education Series

Population Education

UTTAM KUMAR SINGH • K N SUDARSHAN

DISCOVERY PUBLISHING HOUSE
NEW DELHI-110002

First Published - 1996

Reprinted - 2018

ISBN: 978-81-7141-360-7

Population Education

Published by:

DISCOVERY PUBLISHING HOUSE PVT. LTD.
4383/4B, Ansari Road, Darya Ganj
New Delhi-110 002 (India)
Phone: +91-11-23279245, 43596064-65
Fax: +91-11-23253475
E-mail: discoverypublishinghouse@gmail.com
sales@discoverypublishinggroup.com
web: www.discoverypublishinggroup.com

Printed at:
Infinity Imaging Systems
Delhi

Preface

The *DPH Education Handbook* has been created to provide access to information about contemporary topics in education. Practitioners and students at all levels in education have a need to know what is happening today, in addition to historical treatments within the literature.

Each chapter within the Handbook is designed to provide the user with needed "state-of-the-art" information as well as further sources of information. One of the significant features of each chapter is the inclusion of specific programmes, projects and activities so that the researcher can locate human resources as well as the literature.

The handbook will be of use to graduate and post graduate students in education and to practicing teachers, administrators, librarians and planners. The chapters and the further sources of information cited in each book should lead the reader to thousands of people and documents for either research or programme planning purposes.

An effort to achieve universal and effective education is based on a recognition of the rights of students to basic education that enables them to thrive in a complex society, as well as a realization the technological and economic growth is facilitated by increasing the numbers of students, even those with poor academic progresses, who are, in fact successful in learning. Thus, recent and current efforts improve education serve both private and social interests.

This series is addressed to administrators, planners and educators working in the field of education and training with a view to stimulating interest and attention in the areas of education and its related fields. It is also addressed to a growing number of teachers and instructors who will be practitioners in education and who will need to be acquainted with the modern aspects of educational practice and development. Many ideas, generalisations and discussions presented in this series should also prove useful to employing organisations committed to provide training facilities within their establishments—leading to effective mutual participation by institutions and organisations.

The editors wishes to thank the contributors, as well as those organizations that gave permission to publish their extracts, chapters etc.

Editors

Contents

Preface v

1. Population Education 1

2. Ecology of Populations 37

3. Population Environment and Resources 81

4. Social Behaviour and Population Interaction 136

5. Population and Health 185

6. Population and Nutrition 209

7. World Population Growth 244

Index 298

1 Population Education

On 11, July 1987, the world population touched the five billion mark. The world population had been almost stationary at ten million during hundreds and thousands of years of the old stone age. Sometime between 8, 000 B.C. and 6, 000 B.C. man learnt to grow food and so could support a large population. As a result, human population increased to half a billion by A.D. 1650 i.e. an increase by about fifty times in 7, 000 to 9,000 years. In the next 200 years, by 1850, the population doubled and reached its first billion point. But it took about only 100 years to add another billion, and about 45 years to double the population to 4 billion in 1975. And it has taken just 12 years to reach the 5 billion mark in 1987. At the present rate of growth, we will add another billion in the next twelve years. The world population will be over 6 billion by the year 2000 with almost ninety per cent of growth taking place in the developing countries.

According to the 1981 census the population of India was 683.81 million with an annual rate of growth of 2.21 per cent. The United Nations estimates show that the population of India in mid

1988 was 818.78 million and will increase to 1,042.53 million by the end of this century and to 1, 455.57 million on 2025. Today, India ranks second in the world, its total population size being second to China. Her population will almost equal to China in the next 35 years or so. With only 2.42 per cent of the world's land area, India has to support about 15 per cent of the world's population. In comparison to the United States, India is about two-fifty in area but has about two-and-a-half times its population.

What are the implications of this unprecedented increase in population on development and improvement of quality of life of the people.

The population debate

For the past over 200 years, scholars and policy-makers have been debating the question of the relationship between population and development. Controversies have raged about the future of the world because of increasing population and depleting resources. Perhaps the best known controversy is that between the doomsayers' who see the concurrent pressures of population growth, increased demand for resources and environmental degradation as serious threats to the earth's capacity to sustain human population; and the 'cornocopians' who see opportunities rather than problems, who predict with equanimity that human ingenuity, technological advances and efficient distribution systems will usher in a golden tomorrow. There are others who combine different shades of arguments between the tow extreme view points.

One extreme view is held by some people like Ehlrich and Fremlin, Ehlrich in his boo, *The Population Bomb* warns that if growth continues at the present rate for 900 years, there would be some sixty million billion people. This would be about 100 persons for each square yard of the earth's surface, land and sea. The British physicist, J.H. Fremlin, guessed that such a multitudc might be housed in a continuous 2000 storey building covering our entire planet. The space which would be left, after allowing for equipment etc., would be 3 or 4 yards of floor space for each person. Perhaps, he could travel only within a circle of a few hundred yard radius on any floor. However, such a level of population will never come because the biological, physical and social limiting factors will start applying long before the frightening stage, as envisaged by Ehlrich and Fremlin, is reached. 'Growth whether of size or number, is a determinate process, self-limiting. Otherwise, it exceeds the capacity of organization and becomes pathological.

Julian Simon offers a more optimistic picture of the future of the world. According to him 'there is no physical or economic reason why human resourcefulness and enterprise cannot forever continue to respond to impending shortages and existing problems with new expedients that after an adjustment period, leave us better off than before the problem arose. Adding more people will cause us much more problems, but at the same time there will be more people to solve these problems and leave us with the bonus of lower costs and less scarcity in the long run. The bonus applies to such desirable resources as better health, more wilderness, cheaper energy, and a cleaner environment'.

The relationship between population and development was one of the issues on which views were most sharply divided at the Bucharest World Population explosion seriously retarded development ad that measures to reduce birth rates and excess population growth rates would improve the quality of life of individuals and help social and economic aspects of the development process. Many of the developing countries agree with this view, but emphasized that population was not the sole or basic problem. Others were insistent that only rapid development and a restructuring of the international economic system could produce the social conditions necessary for lower birth rate.

Population, consumption styles and development

The increasing affluence with its characteristic consumption-based life-style is equally responsible for the problems of depleting resources and unequal development among countries. Since 1950 the annual growth in global demand for goods and services has been about 4 per cent. The world's population has been growing at a rate of about 2 per cent per annum. The remaining 2 per cent has been absorbed by the rising rate of consumption.

The race among the countries to achieve a

higher rate of economic growth is a significant dimension of the 'resource crisis' problem. Economic growth means more consumption of resources. For example, the annual GNP of western Europe in the late 1960s was about 4.4 per cent which was associated with a 7 per cent in that period was accompanied by a 17. 1 per cent growth in oil consumption. The same situation prevails with regard to the consumption of other resources.

Garrett Hardin's analysis of the 'Tragedy of the Commons has become a classic statement to explain the over-utilization of resources. Using the analogy of the common pasture land of historic English villages, he argues that the carrying capacity of such common resource will be exceeded when individuals act in an economically rational manner. Thus, to maximize immediate welfare, each herdsman places additional cows on the pasture, since the benefits accrue directly to him while the costs of additional grazing are shared with all other herdsmen. In short, the rational herdsman concludes that the only sensible course for him to pursue is to add another animal to his herd. But his is the conclusion reached by each and every rational herdsman sharing a commons. Therein lies the tragedy. Each man is locked into a system that complex him to increase his herd **without limit-in a world that is limited. Ruin is the destination toward which all men rush, each** pursuing his own interest in a society that believes in the freedom of the commons. Freedom in a commons brings ruin to all. In fact, 'Tragedy of the Commons' is analogous to a wider range of complex problems which we are facing today.

There is a great variation among countries in the consumption of different resources. In fact, there is what is called a 'Consumption Explosion' happening mainly in the developed countries . The developed countries with only about 25 per cent of the world's population consume about 75 per cent of the world's resources. The United States, with only 6 per cent of world's population, consumes about one third of the resources. Davis compared consumption of resources by an average Indian and an average American. According to him the average Indian eats his daily few cups of rice or perhaps wheat, draws his bucket of water from the communal well and sleeps in a mud hut. He burns cow dung to cook his rice and warm his feet. His contribution to the destruction of the land and resource is minimal.

An American, on the other hand, can be expected to destroy a piece of land on which he builds a home, garage and driveway. He will contribute his share to the 142 million tons of smoke and fumes, seven million junked cars, 20 million tonnes of paper 48 billion cans and 26 billion bottles, which the overburdened environment must absorb each year.

In 'Indian equivalents, therefore, the population of the United States was about seven billion in 1984. And the rate of growth was even more alarming.

Another dimension to the problem of development has been identified by the Brand Report. It points out that an enormous amount of resources is being diverted for the development of armaments which are being used and will be used for destruction of human beings and earth. The Report says that the annual military bill is about 450 billion US dollars, while expenditure on development accounts for less than 5 per cent of this figure. It eites other examples such as the following :

1. The military expenditure of only half a day would suffice to finance the whole malaria eradication programme of the World Health Organisation.
2. A modern tank costs about one million dollars; that amount could improve storage facilities for 100,000 tonnnes of rice and thus save 4,000 tonnes or more annually: one person can live on just over a pound of rice a day. The same sum of money could provide 1, 000 classrooms for 30,000 children.
3. For the price of one jet fighter one could set up about 40,000 village pharmacies.
4. One-half of one per cent of one year's world military expenditure would pay for all the farm equipment needed to increase food production and approach self sufficiency, eliminating the food deficity of low-income countries by 1990.

In recent years, countries have diverted a

significant proportion of their national resources to defence. This world's military expenditure crossed the trillion dollar mark in 1985. Spending in 1984 was estimated to be about $ 970 billion.

According to the latest assessment of the U.S. Government, Arms Control and Disarmament Agency, NATO and Warsaw Pact countries account for nearly three-fourths of present global defence spending. The growth in real military spending by developed countries increased from an annual rate of under 2 per cent in the 1970s to over 4.5 per cent in 1982-84.

Contrary to this trend of growing military spending by advanced countries, growth in defence expenditure in developing countries slackened from a dramatic 12 per cent in 1972-75 to an estimated 2 per cent in 1982-84.

In 1982, ACDA estimated that the developed states spent $57,000 per member of its armed forces-five times more than the average of $ 10,500 spent on each member of the armed forces of developing countries.

Some third world countries have also been dragged into the mad race of substantially boosting their armaments, sometimes to protect their legitimate or more understandable security interests, but sometimes also for prestige purposes and sometimes on being encouraged by arms-producing countries. Business has been rewarding for both old and new arms suppliers who have spread an incredible destructive capability over the globe. Many developing countries are spending a major portion of their income on defence as compared to other sectors such as health, education, social services etc. It is a terrible irony that the most dynamic and rapid transfer of highly sophisticated equipment and technology from rich to poor countries has been in the machinery of death.

From the foregoing discussion of the problems of increasing population, rising consumption and huge spending on armaments, the understanding of the relationship between population and development becomes highly complex. Unless the value judgement is made as to what a developed society is, it is difficult to determine which changes are part of the development process. Alternatives themselves range from differing political, ideological or social systems.

Some member states of the United Nations system expressed collective concern about the implications of population growth and distribution for development in a declaration, now known as the United Nations Declaration on Population, issued by the Secretary General of the United Nations on Human Rights Day, 10 December, 1966. The countries which sponsored the Declaration and subscribed their signatures to it consisted of three developed countries, Sweden, Finland and Yugoslavia, and nine developing countries, Columbia, India, Korea, Malaysia, Morocco, Nepal, Singapore, Tunisia and the United Arab Republic. There has been no looking back since then. The concern with population problems has become almost universal and a majority of the countries have added their signatures to this Declaration.

Although the relationship between population and development is complex and not yet completely understood, the Report of the State of World Population 1988 says: 'Increasing human demands are damaging the natural resource base-land, water and air-upon which all life depends. High fertility and rapid population growth are contributing to the process. In developing countries, slower growth and more even distribution of population would help to take pressure off agricultural land, energy sources, vital watersheds and forest areas, giving time for governments, the private sector and the international community to evolve strategies for sustainable development. In the poorest areas, the "scissors effect" of poverty and increasing population is slicing away at their ability to sustain human life. Many poor countries with high population growth rats have, in fact, already discovered that they have to run very fast to stay in the same place.

Need for population education

Realizing the negative effect of rapid population growth on development. Many developing countries have launched family planning programmes. The success of family planning programmes in some countries such as China, has been significant in terms of reducing the rate of population growth. However, in a majority of countries, including India, family planning programmes have not been so successful.

There are two main reason *inter alia* for the hidden momentum of population growth in the developing countries. These are (i) the socio-cultural and religious values of the people which influence their fertility behaviour, and (ii) the large young population of these countries. Population change is both biological as well as a socio-cultural phenomenon. The whole process of reproduction leading to the birth of a child is biological. But the decisions behind the birth of a child and the size of family are governed by socio-cultural values, traditions and customs. For example, in most of the developing countries people place a high value on the birth of a son. Similarly, there are many other pro-natalist values which influence the fertility behaviour of the people. In general, socio-cultural values change sluggishly over time through a variety of factors; but one of the most important factors is education. Any coercion in changing the values of the people can backlash and foil all the efforts. There are a number of studies which show a direct relationship between education of the people and their fertility behaviour. For example, a study conducted in Thailand shows that the rural women with five or more years of education bore, on an average, just over half as many children as those with no schooling. Urban women with ten or more years of education bore less than 45 per cent as many children as their counterparts with no schooling.

Similarly, the 1970 census data of the Republic of Korea shows that the average number of children born per woman among those who studied beyond secondary level was significantly lower than among those who never attended school.

In her inaugural address at the First Conference of Asian Forum of Parliamentarians for Population and Development held at New Delhi from 17 to 20 February 1984, Mrs. Indira Gandhi the then Prime Minister of India made a specific reference to the importance of education in inculcating attitudinal and behavioural changes in the people to accept family planning. This should be accompanied by orgnaizational arrangements for contraceptive advice and medical services. She sad:

Young people must be in the vanguard of the movement to restrict population growth and to promote sustained development. In schools and colleges and through non-formal education they must be made conscious of the dynamics of population growth and its implications for their own further will being and that of the nation. Properly planned population education programmes need to be introduced at various levels so that when young people marry, they are fully aware of their responsibility to them selves, to future generations land to society. Every occasion and festival, be it religious or otherwise, where people get together, affords excellent opportunity to reach out to them to explain the importance of these programmes.

In view of the potential of education in

alleviating the problems arising from increasing population, many countries have launched population education programmes at different levels of education in both formal and non-formal sectors during the past decade or so.

Historical perspective

Population education has a relatively short history. The first attempt to voice the need for population in education was made, perhaps, by Ava Myrdal in 1941. In her book *Nation and Family* she tried to convince the United States of America that a conscious population policy was essential to realize the social policy. She emphasized the role of education in the development of new population policy. She, of course, referred to such education as family education. Nothing significant happened with regard to the inclusion of population content in curricula for about two decades. The March 1962 issue of *Teachers College Record,*, Columbia University, carried an article by Warren S. Thomson entitled. 'The Population Explosion' and another article 'Population-Gap in the Curriculum', by Philip M. Hauser. Both of these articles drew attention to the need to include population content in the school curriculum. In 1964, a project to prepare instructional materials related to population education was undertaken at Teachers College, Columbia University, under the leadership of Professor Solan Wayland. The output of this project were two documents entitled *Teaching Population Dynamics,* and *Critical Stages of Reproduction.* These were designed as proto-type materials for the pre-service training of secondary school teachers.

While some efforts were being made at the individual level for introducing population content in the curriculum, the United Nations, particularly UNESCO, took, keen interest and initiative in this direction. The first Director-general of UNESCO, Sir Julian Huxley, in his Annual Report for 1948, emphasized that over-population and with the problems of erosion and depletion of natural resources. Somehow or other, he wrote, 'population must be balanced against resources. Somehow or other, he wrote, 'population must be balanced against resources or civilization will perish. He suggested that UNESCO's task must included educating the peoples of the world to realize the gravity of the problem involved.

UNESCO's General Conference declared in 1968 that the purpose of UNESCO's activities in the field of population should de to promote a better understanding of the serious responsibilities which population growth imposes on individuals, nations and whole international community. In 1970, it authorized the Director General to assist Member States, on request, in the elaboration of population and family planning policies; and in 1972 it recommended that the Director-General promote by means of of education and information, a clearer insight among the public into the nature, causes and consequences of demographic trends. The General Conference of UNESCO at its seventeenth session adopted resolution 1.221 authorizing the Director-General to pursue and undertake activities designed *inter alia* for the promotion of population education.

The Workshop on Population and Family Education, sponsored by the UNESCO Regional office for Education in Asia and held at Bankok in September-October 1970, was a landmark in the history of population education. Educators from thirteen member states in Asia addressed themselves to the task of preparing a statement of objectives for population education, suggesting strategies for organizing programmes, outlining content for incorporation into school curricula in the social sciences and the natural sciences, and preparing a set of draft sample instructional materials in mathematics, science and social studies. A noteworthy outcome of the workshop was that in course of time several of the participants played key roles in developing population programme in their own countries.

In some countries, population education was instituted in response to the recommendation of the World Plan of Action, which stated that government should consider making provision in both the formal and non-formal educational programmes for informing their people on the consequences of existing or alternative fertility behaviour for the well-being of the family, for the educational and psychological development of children and for the general welfare of society, so that an informed and responsible attitude to marriage and reproduction will be promoted.

After initial resistance, the programme of

population education picked up quite fast in the seventies. Five countries in Asia launched national programmes in population education after the 1970 Regional Workshop, with the financial support of the United Nations Fund for Population Activities and technical assistance of UNESCO. By 1988 about twenty-five countries in Asia and the PAcific region had started national population education programmes.

India was, perhaps, the first country to have taken up the task of introducing population education. The Family Planning Association of India presented a memorandum to the Government of Maharashtra, urging that population education be introduced into he educational system of the state. During the same period a 'White Paper' on educational reconstruction was published by the Maharashtra Government in April 1988. The proposal was based on the firm conviction that one of the important ways in which the educational system can be made a 'powerful instrument of national development' was by providing a basic understanding of the dynamics of population growth and how did it affect the daily lives of the people an national welfare. The memorandum, however, made it clear that teaching about population control did not mean teaching young people about specific birth control methods and techniques, nor did it include sex education.

The first National Seminar on Population Education held in 1969 at Bombay set the space for the introduction of population education into the school system. Since 1980, population education has been launched as a national programme under the banner of the National Population Education Programme but the Ministry of Education with the financial assistance of UNFPA and technical assistance of programme. The NPEP is executed by the NCERT and, during its first cycle, had sought to institutionalize population education in the formal school and teacher training systems. The programme was expanded to non-formal education, adult education and universities during the Seventh Five Year plan.

Conceptualizing population education

Since the population education programme was initiated to supplement the family planning programme, it is sometimes misunderstood, both within and outside the educational system, as another name for sex education and/or family planning education. This misconception has been one of the hurdles in starting population education programmes in some countries. Cultural variations have determined differences in the concept and scope of population education programmes in different geographical regions. In many countries in Asia and the Pacific region there is a cultural and religious resistance to include any kind of family planning or sex education component in school curricula. Sex education is still considered 'untouchable' in many countries in Asia, although some countries such as the Republic of Korea and the Philippines have included family planning and sexuality as a part of population education curriculum in schools. In Fiji, sex education is a major component of family life education.

On the other hand, some Latin American countries place major emphasis on sex education because of the need felt for the individual to understand himself on herself as a sexual being, which is a prerequisite to the development of responsible parenthood. It should, however, be noted that in Latin America and to a lesser degree in Francophone Africa, the term sex education is used to suggest a broader range of activities. There, 'sex education' may be the most suitable term for what has been called in Asia 'population education.

Conceptualization of population education is rather a question of emphasis, rooted in complex cultural and historical differences. The situation is not expected to remain static. There are already signs of change in the concept and scope of population education in some countreis. Although some countries do not openly accept any kind of sex education or family planning education in schools, they do realize the need for including some content related to these areas in the population education curriculum. A number of surveys recently conducted in some countries in Asia vouch to this change in the perception of and their acceptance to include sex education related contents in the framework of population education.

The concept and scope of population education

also differs with target group. Although opinions may differ with regard to the nature and content of population education for the children, there is little difference of opinion so far as the population education programme for youth and adults is concerned. The information on sex and family life is of immediate relevance to this group.

Defining population education

Given the cultural diversities and different target groups, it may be difficult to give one definition of population education which can be universally accepted. Definitions also differ in the specific behavioural outcomes which they specify, such as acceptance of a small family norm while others adopt a non-directive approach. The assertion that 'a small family is a happy family' is not universally true for there are many instances of bigger families being happy families. The pursuit of such an objective may have psychological implications for children who come from larger families.

Inspite of the difficulties in the perception of population education, many individuals and many conferences have tried to give a definition of population education.

Population education is an educational programme which provides for a study of the population situation in the family country, nation and world with the purpose of development in the students of rational and responsible attitude and behaviour towards that situation.

Population education is 'an educational programme which helps learners to understand the inter-relationship of population dynamics and other factors of quality of life and to make informed and rational decisions with regard to population related behaviours with the purpose of improving the quality of life of himself, his family, community, nation and the world'.

The above two definitions will give an idea of the change in the thrust and nature of population education over the past decade. The first definition focuses on the development of attitudes and behaviours towards the population situation the main objective being population control. The second definition aims at understanding the inter-relationship of various factors of quality of life and making rational decisions for its improvement. Population dynamics is one of the factors in the whole process of improvement of quality of life.

The concept of population education as stated in the second definition, according to which the main goal of population is to improve the quality of life of the people at the micro-and macro-levels.

There are a variety of factors which affect the achievement of the desired quality of life. These include population dynamics, socio-political system, process of development, availability of resources and the existing levels of living of the people. It should be noted that population dynamics is *one of the factors* of quality of life which affects other factors and is in turn affected by them. This means that controlling population growth does not automatically ensure improvement in the quality of life of the people. There are some countries in Asia which illustrate this point. For example, the Republic of South Korea had a population growth of about 2 per cent during 1970s but achieved a very high rate of economic growth, about 10 per cent per annum during the past over a decade. On the other hand, there were many countries with the same or lower rate of population growth but which showed a poor rate of economic growth. This, however, does not mean that a high rate of population increase in developing countries will not affect their development. In fact, countries with large populations and a high rate of population growth have to invest a greater share of their resources in meeting the basic demands of the increasing population. With the result, very little resources are left improving the quality of life of the people.

The concept of quality of life

Quality of life is a very complex concept and perceived and interpreted differently by different people depending upon their socio-cultural and religious back ground, personal preferences and their philosophy of life. Perceived qualities of life depend on culture and internalized values and vary like other human requirements. For one society collective religious practices or communal life patterns may be primary, for others, individually oriented work or recreative pursuits may rank higher. Some societies prize tradition and continuity as important aspects of social quality whilst others place a high premium on innovation and modernity. Societies such as Japan may seek a balance of both tradition and modernity. Some Muslim countries have opted for a renaissance of its Islamic culture, whilst other countries have sought their qualitative goals in different ways. Developing nations may need strong assertion and acceptance of their cultural and political identity as a prerequisite for their qualitative development.

It would be impossible to set standards of quality for human beings in absolute terms. But one can suggest that people should have access to a range of options and alternatives which would allow them to select those particular qualities they desire. Various attempts have been made to define the quality of life, ranging from individual subjective evaluations to large-scale cross-national surveys. The quality of life is the sense of being pleased or satisfied with those life-elements that are most important to a person. In addition, quality is the sense of being pleased with what one has. Although satisfaction, happiness, or pleasure is the central element in this definition, it should not be seen as a momentary state of happiness or pleasure but rather a long-run sense of happiness. It is perhaps best expressed as a sense of fullness or completeness of life. The quality of life involves the satisfaction sense of fullness or completeness of life. The quality of life involves the satisfaction of the emotional needs and social aspirations of the community or society as well as the society's ability to meet the basic needs of food, energy, space, housing, etc., by itself.

One of the criteria which can be applied to assess the standard of living or the quality of life may be the degree to which a society is stable or can live in harmony with nature without endangering itself or the environment for an indefinite period of time. One could identify four principal conditions of a stable society, a society that to all intents and purposes can be sustained indefinitely while giving optimum satisfaction to its members. These are (i) minimum disruption of ecological processes; (ii) maximum conservation of material and energy or an economy of stock rather than flow; (iii) a population in which the recruitment equals the loss; and (iv) a social system in which the individual can enjoy, rather than be restricted by the first three conditions.

Objectives of population education.

The population education programmes in different countries have been launched with different emphases depending upon political, social and cultural values of the society. Some countries are explicit about contributing to decreasing population growth rate. Other countries talk in general terms such as the impact of rapid population growth rate on quality of life. A couple of countries focus on family life education and at least two country projects are concerned with population distribution. These are briefly discussed below.

Decreasing the rate of population growth

China, Tahiland and Viet Nam are quite explicit in focussing on control limitation of the rate of population growth, as shown by their long-range objectives.

China 'To contribute to the implementation of the overall Government Population Polity of reducing the rate of population growth to achieve zero population growth by the year 2000.'

Thailand: 'To help Thai people to make critical and rational decisions, pertaining to population and family planning matters. The programme hopes to contribute to the Government's effort to cut down the rapid rate of population increase'.

Viet Nam: 'To contribute to the realization of the population policy, i.e. to create awareness, understanding and support to effort to reduce population growth rate and to redistribute the country's population'.

Family life education

The long range objectives of two out-of-school country projects in Afghanistan and Malaysia are centred on family-life education.

Afghanistan: To design and organize functional literacy programmes for rural and urban women related to family health, better family living and family guidance.

Malaysia. To strengthen the family planning component of the family development programme by broadening its scope to family life education emphasizing, besides, family planning, the need for the improvement of quality of life of the individual, family and community, and in this way to contribute to the achievement of general objectives of the family development programme.'

Population distribution

One country project, that of Viet Nam, included population redistribution in its statement of long-range objectives as already stated in the preceding section.

In addition, although not explicitly made a part of the long range objectives, the population education programmes in Indonesia are concerned with population redistribution. The project authorities very often speak of uneven distribution of population as one among the serious population problems of the country, whereby 63.8 per cent of the total land area of the country. The long-range objective of the Sri Lanka project also made reference to 'the impact of population growth and distribution on the quality of life.'

Quality of life

By and large, the long-range objectives of many country projects are mainly concerned with (i) an understanding of the interrelationship of population change and socio-economic development, as well as aspects of quality of life; and (ii) an understanding of the population situation in the family, community, nation and the world, for the purpose of developing in students and out-of-school youth and adults rational and responsible attitudes and behaviour in response to population problems and issues deemed necessary to enhance the people's quality of life.

Although countries differ in respect of specific objectives of their population education programmes, the general objectives are more or less the same. The following general objectives could very well represent the nature of population education.

To enable learners to acquire the knowledge, skills, attitudes and values necessary (a) to understand and (b) to evaluate the prevailing population situation, the dynamic forces which have shaped it and the effect it will have on the present and future welfare of themselves, their families, communities, societies, nations and the world; (c) to make conscious and informed decisions; and (d) to respond to population situations and problems in a conscious and informed manner.

In view of different socio-cultural backgrounds and population policies of the countries, the specific objectives of population education programmes are different. The specific objectives are also different for different grade levels and target groups. It will, therefore, not be worthwhile to list the specific objectives of population education. The following can be the major general objectives of population education.

1. To develop awareness and understanding about:
   - (a) population situation-national and world;
   - (b) basic demographic concepts and theories;
   - (c) process of population change;
   - (d) determinants of population change;

(e) concepts of quality of life in different socio-cultural settings;

(f) inter-relationship between population change and different aspects of quality of life at the micro-and macro-levels;

(g) consumption explosion ad its implications on quality of life for others;

(h) human reproduction, eugenics and family welfare; and

(i) population policies, plans and programmes.

2. To develop the ability to assess the quality-of-life implications in relation to population change and consumption of resources, now and in the future, for oneself, one's community, national and the world.

3. To develop rational attitudes, values and skills for taking responsible decisions and actions regarding population-related issues and improvement of quality of life.

Some issues and trends in population education

Population education being a value-laden area, one is bound to deal with many issues in implementing this programme. These issues arise because of the differences in the social, cultural, religious, economic and political systems and values of the people. Most of the values are so deep-rooted in the socio-cultural milieu of the people that a concerted and continuous effort is needed to change them. During the last decade or so countries with population education programmes have developed a rich experience in dealing with these issues and as a result new trends in the implementational of population education programmes are emerging. Some of the issues trends are discussed here.

Issues

Conceptual: The goals of most population education programmes generally refer to developing understanding, awareness, attitudes and responsible and informed decision-making and behaviour for improving the quality of life as the end-product of the education activity. Most goal statements are somewhat ambiguous and do not specify the nature of the behaviour to be achieved.

In view of the controversial nature of population education, a number of issues keep coming up. These include issues like: What is population education? How does it differ form family planning and/or sex education? Does population education hold better prospect for success than family planning? What is the guarantee that the non-prescriptive approach in population education will be more effective than the prescriptive approach? What do we mean by quality of life? How far is it true that population education will help in improving the quality of life at the micro and macro-levels?

Curriculum: Different approaches for developing curricula in population education have been used by different countries. Population education being of recent origin, has no clearly marked content boundaries. It is inter-disciplinary in nature and related to various subjects. The problem of an already overcrowded curriculum makes it difficult to establish population education as an independent subject in schools. The countries have, therefore used the integration approach to include population education concepts in different subject areas. The curricula in population education n countries with population education programmes have been developed to suit tho socio-cultural as well as educational needs of the more or less the same, there are differences in the immediate objectives, content areas, subjects of integration as well as modalities and approaches for materials development. for example, the curricula in population education of the Republic of Korea and the Philippines include contents relating to sexuality and family planning whereas other countries have avoided including them because of socio-cultural factors.

In many countries population education content has been integrated in as many as six or seven subjects. The result is that population education content gets so dispersed and diffused that it looses its focus and identity.

Some issues related to curriculum development in population education are: At what stage should population education be introduced? In view of the already heavy curriculum what approach should be used to introduce population education in the curriculum? What content should be included at different grade levels? What should be the minimum learning contents for different categories of audiences? How does one ensure integration of adequate population education content into curricula and textbooks?

Methodologies of Teaching. A variety of methodologies have been suggested for teaching population education but, keeping the nature of the subject in view, discovery-oriented or inquiry approach, values clarification and role-playing are recommended for teaching population education. The studies on teaching methodologies are inconclusive as to their relative effectiveness.

The following are some issues related to methodologies to teaching: Which are the effective methods in teaching population education? What is the possibility of using discovery or inquiry approach in teaching population education in view of the existing situations and constraints in schools. Isn't it a contradiction to expect teachers to use the discovery or problem-solving approach when they use traditional methods of teaching the subjects into which population education has been integrated?

Training: Training is one of the important components of all population education programmes. But it has also been the most difficult problem for the countries because of the enormous number of teachers and other persons who need to be trained within the financial and time constraints. The countries which have already launched national population education programmes have experimented with different strategies of training in addition to face-to-face training. Each strategy has its merits and demerits. There is as yet no empirical study conducted which can vouch for or recommend one or the other strategy. The countries have to decide themselves which strategy or combination of strategies could be effective in achieving the planned objectives of the training programmes as per their needs, available resources and constraints.

One is faced with the following issues in the training of personnel: What are the alternatives to face-to-face training to reach the maximum number of teachers and other personnel within a reasonable time, without sacrificing quality of training?

What formative and summative evaluation could be used to assess and ensure effectiveness of training programmes? What strategies of in-service training are cost-effective? What should be the duration of training for different categories of personnel in order to be effective? What approach (es) should be used for introducing population education in the pre-service training of teachers?

Evaluation and research: This is one of the weak areas in most of the national population education programmes. Although most of the projects have some kind of in-built evaluation process of curriculum, materials and training programmes, there have been very few systematic and comprehensive evaluation studies on the impact of the programme on the target audiences.

Only some programmes during the past three to four years have initiated comprehensive and longitudinal studies to evaluate the impact of the programme.

Population education deals not only with the cognitive domain but even more importantly with the effective domain i.e. with attitudes, appreciations and values which are not easy to assess. In the absence of any reliable tool of evaluation, it would be difficult to say whether the objectives of population education have been achieved or not. The problem of evaluation is further complicated by the fact that invariably population education content has been integrated into different subjects.

There seems to be a dearth of research in the substantive and methodological areas in population education. However, where there are researches, one wonders if they are being utilized as bases for programming different aspects of population education.

In the absence of systematic evaluation and research and in the light of the problems discussed, can we say the changes in population-related attitudes and values are due to population education programmes? To what extent would we be correct in attributing a reduction in the fertility rate in a community or country to its population education programme? How then do we justify the population education programme vis-a-vis the family planning programme? What then are the most appropriate ways of evaluating the impact of population education on the knowledge, attitudes and behaviour of different target audiences?

Operational: Two types of operational models are being used by different countries for implementing population education programmes. In some countries the population education projects are a part of the functions of Curriculum Development Centres. In others, they are separate projects under the Ministry of Education. These projects work in close collaboration with the curriculum development bodies and other concerned departments.

Both of these models have their merits and demerits. The first model is however, favoured over the second model because of its administrative and operational merits, and because it is more successful in integrating population education content in different school subjects as well as in the in-service training of teachers.

Institutionalization: The ultimate aim of population education is its institutionalization in the education system of the country. This process of institutionalization involves the following:

(a) Population education content becomes an integral part of the curriculum and textbooks, either as a separate subject or as integrated into existing subjects.

(b) Population education is incorporated as one of the areas of study in the pre-service teacher training institutions.

(c) Questions on population education are included in the public examinations.

(d) Population education is also introduced at the tertiary level of education as well as in non-formal and adult education programmes.

A close look at population education programmes in Asia and the Pacific region reveals that, although, some of these national programmes are a decade old, they have a long way to go before it can be said that population education is fully institutionalized in their education systems. Most of them are still passing through a transition period. This is because of the number of issues and problems of curriculum, integration into textbooks, training of teachers and other personnel, incorporation of population education in training institutions, financial constraints, etc.

Trends

The following trends have emerged during the past decade:

1. Population education is considered by most countries to be an integral part of their national development plans and education policies.

2. Although virtually all population education programmes espouse an open-ended, non-prescriptive approach in their goals and objectives, the content as well as approach is, often implicitly and sometimes explicitly, more directed towards the specific goal of promoting a small family norm. The funding agencies

also want to see the effect of population education programmes on the reproductive behaviour of the target audience. This is more true for the out-of-school youth and adults.

3. Population education is considered relevant, not only by the countries with large populations, but also by countries with small populations with high rates of population growth.

4. Although population education is being introduced at all levels of school education, priority is being given to the middle and secondary levels.

5. The scope and content is being broadened to include relating to sex education, family life education, responsible parenthood, adolescent fertility, delayed marriage and population related beliefs and values.

6. A smaller number of subjects, two or three, is selected for integrating population education concepts instead of five or more subjects.

7. In addition to integrating population education into the existing curriculum, a separate elective/required course is also being offered at the secondary level in some countries.

8. Some efforts are being made to utilize research studies on students' and teachers' knowledge, attitudes, and values concerning population matters for preparing curriculum and instructional materials.

9. Population education is offered as separate elective/required courses at teachers training colleges in some countries. It is also being offered as one of the specializations at the post graduate level by the Facilities of Education.

10. The need and importance of population education is being increasingly recognized by the universities and colleges and it is, therefore, being offered as an interdisciplinary elective or required course and /or in the form of extension lectures for the undergraduate students.

11. A variety of innovative strategies for the in-service training of teachers is being used, such as peer training, mobile training, self-instructional training, distance training etc., in addition to the traditional face-to-face training.

12. Effective methodologies of teaching, such as discovery or inquiry, role playing, simulation, games, etc., are being increasingly recognized and given serious trials.

13. In order to effectively monitor and co-ordinate the programme, coordination or steering committees in population education have been set up at the national, provincial and district levels in many countries.

14. Questions on population education are being included in the public examinations.

15. Longitudinal studies are being undertaken as a part of the programme in order to evaluate the impact of the programme on target audience.

2 Ecology of Populations

Populations are fundamental units in ecology, as important to the ecologist as are tissues and organs to the anatomist and physiologist. They may be thought of as major components of communities and ecosystems, just a tissues and organs are major components of individual organisms while tissues and organs are composed of individuals in functional groups.

A population is a group of living individuals set in a frame-that is limited and defined in respect to both time and space. Also population is an interacting, or potentially interacting group of individuals usually of the same species. It may be the population of ants in an ant hill, the population of salmon in a river, the population of a deer in a state and so forth. Biologically, a population should have some natural boundaries as is the ants in an ant hill, but the term is often used with artificial boundaries in mind, as in referring to the population of deer in a state. A state might have several biological population of deer, but for economic or political consideration it is convenient to put them together. The human population representing varied ethnic religious or economic groups these population within one nation might have different characteristics.

Population Attributes

In the initial study of populaion it is helpful to recognize certain attribute of population which distinguish them from individual organisms like organisms have a structural organization, a functional unity, and a pattern of growth and development unlike individuals they have group attributes and statistical properties that no single individual possess. The more important of these population characteristics or group attributes are as follows,

Density: Population size in relation to unit of space.

Birth rate: or more broadly natality the rate at which new individuals are added to the population by reproduction.

Death rate: or mortality rate: The rate at which individuals are lost by death.

Dispersal: The rate at which individuals immigrate into the population and emigrate out of the population.

Population growth rate: or growth form. The net result of natality mortality & dispersal.

Dispersion: The way in which individuals are distributed in space, generally in one or more the following patterns:

i) Random distribution, in which probability of an individual occurring in any one part is the same as the probability of it occuring at any other part.

ii) Union distribution, in which components occur more regularly than random such as corn in a cornfield.

iii) Clumped distribution (the most common in nature) in which individuals or other components are more irregular than random as for example a clump of plants arising from vegetative reproduction, a flock of bird, of people in a city.

Age distribution: The proportion of individuals of different ages in the group.

Genetic characteristics especially applicable to population ecology as for example, adaptiveness reproductive fitness and persistence.

Individual organisms are born, have age, grow and die but such characteristic as birth rate, death rate, density and other listed above are meaningful only at the group level. If we are to understand thoroughly the ecology of a species, we must study and measure these population group characteristics as well as know the life history and identifying features of the species. And of course, we all must be concerned about the vital statistics of human population.

The detailed information of some of the population attributes are given below.

Population Sizes

Some of the most important aspects of population

structure are population size, density, spatial distribution age and sex rates, breeding structure and social organization. Population sizes may vary from a few individuals to millions of individuals. The population of whooping cranes (Grus American) numbers about 50 individuals a single group of birds barely clining to existence. Other rare and endangered species around the world also represent very small populations. The world's population of the Indian lion (Panthera Ieo) numbers less than 200 individuals living in the Gir forest of western India. The California condor (Gymonogyps californicus), golden marmoset (Leontideus rosalia) Javan rhinoceros (Didermocerus sumatrensis) orangutan (Pongo pygmaeus), Gray jungle fowl (Gallus sonnerati) and many other species are now represented by small remnant populations wavering on the edge between life and death.

At the other extreme, the world contains many species of tremendous abundance. A population of starlings in a sigle winter flocking roost in eastern United States may number 5 million birds. The white-tailed deer population of Pennsylvania was estimated in 1946 to contain 1 million deer; the rhesus monkey population of one province in northern India was estimated in 1960 to contain between 800,000 and 1 million monkeys (it now probably contains less than half that number); the Norway rat population of Baltimore was estimated in World War II at 400,000; and the bison population of the Great Plains was estimated to contain 60 million individuals in the early nineteenth century, though by the 1890's the bison population had crashed to less than 600 through the greed and disruptive influence of man.

Population estimates

These figures raise the question; of course as to how such data are obtained, and this is a large and complicated subject in itself. Censusing wild animal population is fraught with many difficulties of sampling error and statistical bias. Occasionally direct counts are possible as in aerial photographs of big game herds or sea bird colonies, but for most animals this is impossible and various kinds of sampling methods must be employed. Most animals are not readily visible because of their behavior and habitat, or because they exist in such abundance or scarcity that they cannot be readily counted. It therefore becomes necessary to estimate numbers through programs of capture and resembling. With many animals systematic program of capture-mark-recapture has been helpful in obtaining estimates of abundance. The ratio of marked to unmarked animals in subsequent trapping runs provides a population estimate known as the Lincoln Index. If, for example one is studying a resident bird or rodent population in a forest, and succeeds in capturing and banading 100 individuals all of which are released, and then if on a second trapping program, one again catches 100 animals of which 20 were previously banded one would estimate the total original population at 500 animals. This is based on the Lincoln Index ratio which may be written:

$$\frac{P_1}{M_1} = \frac{T_2}{M_2}$$

Where P equals the unknown population, M_1 equals the total number of individuals marked in the first capture period, T_2 equals the total number of individuals captured in the second capture period, and M_2 equals the number of those in the second capture period which were marked. The validity of the method involves several major assumptions: (1) that the marked animals mix randomly in the population, and (2) that the probability of recapture is the same for each individual regardless of whether or not it is marked, and (3) that there be no immigration or emigration; death or births between the sampling periods. Actually, these conditions are rarely attained in natural populations. Many studies on birds and mammals have shown that some individuals are easily captured whereas others are rarely captured. There are thus "trap-happy" individuals and "trap shy" individuals. In some species, one experience with trapping on the part of an individual animal may reduce the probability of subsequent recapture, whereas in others it may enhance it. Such behavior patterns bias the data and reduce the value of the population estimates made with this method. Also, birth, death, immigration and emigration are often continuous processes within populations, so their effect can rarely be eliminated entirely.

Nonetheless, the Lincoln Index approaches

validity in certain cases. It can be a helpful tool for population estimates, particularly in the following cases: (1) if a capture method is available which is relatively nonselective and random in its action, (2) if a relatively confined population is available so that emigration and immigration do not occur, as an island population, a woodland population surrounded by forest, an oasis , etc., (3) if the population can be sampled at a time when it is relatively stable, not reproducing during the sampling period, and not migrating. Under these circumstances, capture-mark-recapture technique can produce the best available result on certain animal populations.

Another method of estimating animal population size is based on a change in sex ration before and after a known harvest of one sex has been removed. This has been called the Kelker Ratio, and has been used in the estimation of deer, pheasants, and other wildlife populations where hunting statistics are available. In a study of California deer by Dasmann (1952), the sex ratio observed before the hunting season was 74 bucks to 139 does, and after the hunting season in the same area it was 50 bucks to 139 does. The harvest in the hunting season was known to be 246 bucks. Hence the removal of 246 bucks population should be in the same proportion to the original sex ratio as the total buck harvest was to the change in sex ratios produced by the harvest. Thus, the following delker formula was applied to calculate to total population of bucks.

$$\frac{S_1}{P_1} = \frac{S_1 - S_2}{H}$$

Where S_1 equals the pre=hunting sex ratio, P_1 equals the pre-hunting buck population, S_2 equals the post-hunting sex ratio (therefore S_1—S_2 equals the change in sex ratio during the hunt), and H equals the total harvest.

One can readily see some of the observational problems and potential biases in the Kelker Ratio as the Lincoln Index. The Kelker Ratio assumes that the observations of sex ratios before and after harvests are equivalent. It the buck become shyer than the does and are harder to observe after the hunt, this enters a major bias. It is essential that the field ecologist be fully experienced and knowledgeable in the habits of the animal he is studying before he applies these population estimation techniques. He can then recognize the sampling problems and possible sources of error. If reasonably unbiased sample estimates are obtained, it is then important to subject them to statistical treatments such as standard error calculations, or analyses of variance to evaluate the sampling errors which might occur by chance alone. It is thus important for ecologist and statisticians to work closely together in population studies.

Population Density

Population density is an important aspect of both population size and distribution. In many populations, the precise boundaries of the population are unknown. Though the distributional limits of the species may be recognized each species usually consists of several populations. The essential feature which distinguishes a population is whether or not the individuals are potentially interactive, or potentially interbreeding. If a species consists of two or more discrete aggregations, which do not interact or influence each other these aggregations can then be considered populations. If this condition persists over an extended period of time, different races, subspecies and even species may emerge as gene frequencies change and evolution occurs. Since populational boundaries are often unknown the most practical description of population abundance is frequently in terms of densities.

As an example many ecologic studies of small rodents have shown population densities usually in the range of 0.5 to 20 animals per acre. But (1940) showed population densities of the deer mouse (Peromyscus leucopus)in southern Michigan woodlots to range from 3.08 to 10.32 individuals per acre, Blair (1951) estimated the population density of beach mice or old field mice (Peromyscus polionotus) to range from 0.83 to 1.41 individuals per acre. Ashby (1967) estimated population densities of the bank vote (Clethrionomy glaeolus) a relative of the meadow mouse, to run as high as 17 to 18 individuals per acre in central England.

An important consideration, which will be emphasized later, is that many populations fluctuate widely in density and size in the course of natural events. Occasionally small mammal populations reach amazingly high densities. In California, Krebs (1966) described a meadow mouse or vole population (Microtus Californicus) which achieved a density of 150 to 300 individuals per acre in a relatively small area, and Parson (1963) described a population of house mice in California which increased from a density of less than 5 mice per acre to 300 mice per acre within 6 months. At these high levels, or course, rodents can become agricultural problem and can precipitate economic losses of crops or stored food products. Splitte (1968) has estimated that wild rats (Bandicota bengalensis) in Calcutta grain storage warehouses may achieve densities of one rat per sequare meter, equivalent to 4,000 per acre. These represent extreme concentrations, or course, but they indicate the population potential of some species.

Spatial Distribution

Another important consideration in concepts of both population size and density is the spatial distribution of individuals. Spatial distribution involves a fascinating interplay of behavioral and ecologic factors, and is a prime example of the inseparable tie between behavior and ecology. We have been speaking of population densities as though animals were randomly distributed. This is rarely true, and it is much more common for population to be clumped and nonrandomly distributed.

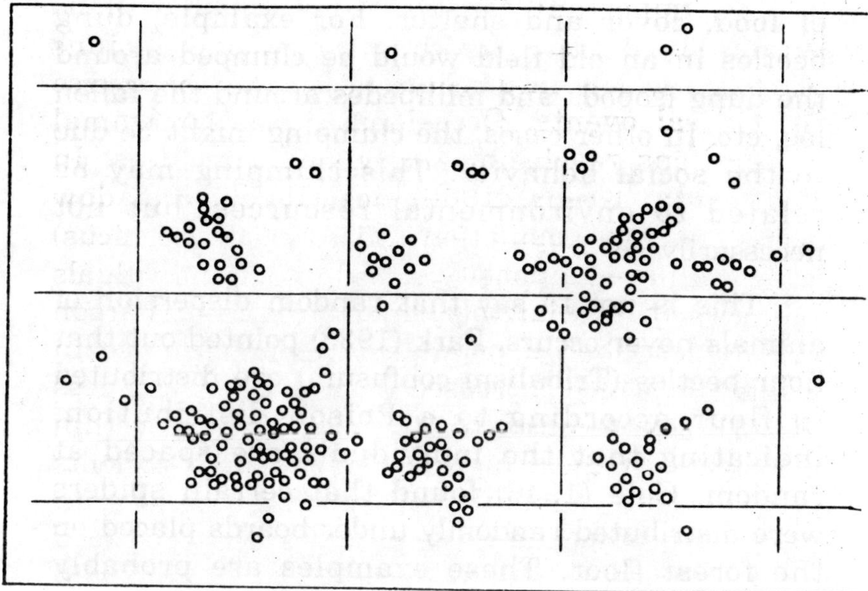

Fig. 1 Typical pattern of spatial distribution of individuals within a population. (The dimensional units of this diagram are entirely hypothetical. They might be millimeters or micra in the case of microorganisma; inches or feet in the case of soil invertebrates; miles in the case of birds or mammals; hundreds of miles in the case of whales.)

A typical pattern of spatial distribution within a population is shown in Figure 1. This might accurately portray the distribution of insects in an old field, isopods or millipedes in aforest, nesting birds or prairie dogs in a grassland, baboons in a savannah, fish in a lake, or even plankton in the sea. The reason for such clumping or nonrandom distribution might be numerous. In some cases clumping would be attributable to the heterogeneity of the environment the distribution of food, cover and shelter. For example, dung beetles in an old field would be clumped around the dung isopods and millipedes around the fallen log, etc. In other cases, the clumping might be due to the social behavior. This clumping may be related to environmental resources, but not necessarily so.

This is not to say that random dispersion of animals never occurs. Park (1933) pointed out that flour beetles (Tribalism confusum) are distributed in flour according to a Poison distribution, indicating that the individuals are spaced at random. Cole (1946) found that certain spiders were distributed randomly under boards placed on the forest floor. These examples are probably exceptions to the general rule, and they are most likely attributable to either the homogeneous or artificial nature of the environment in each case. For purposes of generalization it can be stated with reasonable assurance that most animals and many plants in natural environments show a clumped or nonrandom pattern of distribution.

Sex ratios and age structures

It is obvious that animals within a population differ in a number of ways: sex, age, breeding condition health, physical condition and social status. Demography, or the numerical analysis of populations, is concerned with the sex, age and breeding condition of the population. Medical science and epistemology are primarily concerned with the health and physical condition of the population and behavioural science is primarily concerned with the social and behavioral states within the population.

In most vertebrate populations primary sex ratios at hatching or birth approach 50 percent male and 50 percent female. In some forms, there is a slight deviation from this; in man, for example sex ratio at birth is closer to 52 percent male, and this is true for rabbits cattle and many birds. In domestic chickens, sheep and horses, sex ratios at birth or hatching are usually closer to 49 percent male. The secondary sex ratios or adult sex ratios of many vertebrates show greater diviations, however. In the Alaskan fur seal one adult bull may dominate a breeding group of 30 females. Wheras the total adult male sex ration is greater than 3 percent the excess adult males are on the periphery of the breeding grounds, they are essentially surplus, and they suffer substa-ntially higher mortality. In most primate populations, adult females out number adult males two or three to one. Apparently males have higher mortality rates throughout life than females have higher mortality rates than males, particularly during the nesting season. In waterfowl and gallinaceous birds, for example male often outnumber females. The sex ratio of blue-winged seal (Querquedula discors) in fall and winter flocks averaged 59 percent males in a sample of 5,090 birds and in the early summer breeding population of mallards (Anas platyrhynchos) and pintail (Anas acuta) in Manitoba, males may outnumber females 4 or 5 to 1.

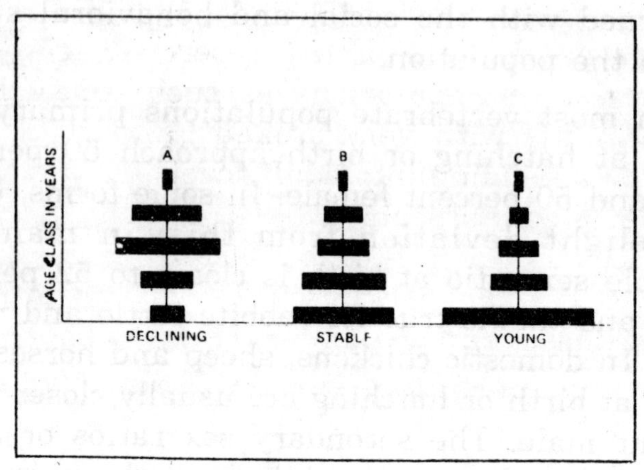

Fig. 2 Theoretical age pyramids representing populations with low, medium, and high percentages of young individuals

Age ratios represent another important element of population structure, and one that is also particularly valuable in analyzing populations dynamics Figure 2 shows age structure of populations in terms of three basis types: (A) a declining population, with a low percentage of young in the population (B) a stable population with a large percentage of young than adults, and (C) an increasing population, with a very large percentage of young. The exact shape and proportions of these age pyramids are a function of natality, mortality and population turnover. Some populations characteri-stically have tremendous production of sex cells and youngs with massive morality of young. The Pacific herring, for example produces 8,000 eggs per famale per season, of which 95 percent hatch but only 0.1 percent survive to maturity. The female shad lays from 30,000 to 100,000 eggs per female per season, and less than 0.1 percent grow into mature fishes. Populations as such would have age pyramids with very broaad bases with tiny segments ascending into adult levels. At the other extreme, elephants and whales usually produce only one young per female every few years, and they would have age pyramids with relatively narrow bases and expanded adult proportions. That is, the majority of animals in the population would be adults.

Figure 3 shows population age structure data on rhesus monkey populations. Rhesus populations in India show different age structures in different habitats. In roadside habitats and villages, where juvenile rhesus monkey (1 to 3 year of age, postweaned but preadult) are trapped for export for use in biomedical research and pharmaceutical production throughout the world, there is a conspicuous juvenile "gap" that is, an unnatural shortage of these individuals. These populations have been declining throughout the 1950's and 1960's at the rate of approximately 5 percent per year, as India has exported any where from 40,000 to over 100,000 rhesus monkey per year, primarily juveniles. In temples where rhesus monkeys are protected to a certain extent for religious reasons, and in forests where they can escape trapping more successfully age structure of an island population of rhesus monkeys on Cayo Santiago Island off the eastern coast of Puerto Rico is also shown. This population has been fed and protected by

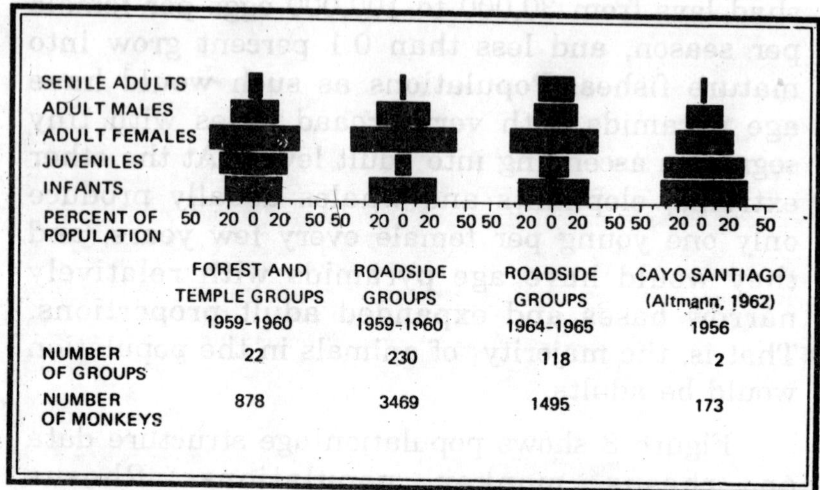

Fig.3 Age structures of rhesus populations.

a governmental research program of the National Institutes of Health, and it shows a broad base of infants and juveniles. This population was increasing at the rate of 16 percent per year in the early 1960's and gave a good indication of the natural tendency of primate populations to increase if protected in a satisfactory habitat.

Life tables

Life tables represent tabular data on age structures of populations, and they also provide information on mortality rates and longvity patterns. The essential data of a life table may be of two basic types: (1) census data on a population with accurate counts of the numbers of individuals in each age category, (2)mortality data on the number of individuals of each age group dying in a given period of years. From such data, surviviorship and longevity can be calculated Insurance companies use life table statistics on human populations to estimate the probability or death at each age group, and from these data they establish rates for life insurance.

Life tables provide ecologists with essential information for the management of animal population. They pinpoint mortality patterns, indicating when deaths occur and how many. If one finds abnormally high mortality occurring in infancy, adolescence, or early adulthood, it may suggest specific management procedures to alleviate this mortality. Excessive infant mortality, for example, may be associated with inadequate food for young animals, or inadequate cover by which they can escape predators, or improper patterns of parental care due to behavioral disturbances within the adult population. Excessive adult mortality might indicate shortage of adult food supplies, infectious diseases or parasitic burdens which become more severe in adulthood, or possibly excessive crowding during the reproductive period so that sexual fighting becomes violent. Thus, life data provide important clues for more detailed study. They seldom give the final answers on why or how certain events occur, but they form the essential starting point of what is happening in a population.

In summary, we have noted that populations may be studied in both anatomical and physiological terms. That is, we may analyze the structure of a population in terms of numbers, density, spatial distribution, sex and age ratios, and other descriptive qualities. Similarly, we may analyze patterns, movements, and other dynamic attributes. The ultimate objectives are to understand the organization of populations and their vital processes. As we see more and more populations getting out of balance, and going toward extremes of great abundance or great rarity and extinction, such understanding has now become critical to human affairs and the quality of life on earth.

Population theories

The question of population has occupied the attention of state men and philosophers since ancient times. But it is only recently that attempts have been made to investigate systematically the cause of population change and the specific ways in which population dynamics influence human welfare.

Plato and Aristotle were interested in the question of population size in the context of a city-state. To them the optimum size of the population was that is with which man's potentialities could be fully developed and his "highest good" realized. Thus was possible when the population range was enough to be economically self-sufficient and capable of defending itself, but not too large for constitutional government. Plato specified 5,040 as the number of citizens "most likely to be useful to all cities".

European authors on population during the early modern and the medieval periods favoured a growing population. The discovery of the New World, the increase of commerce between Europe and Asia, and the rise of national state brought about some changes in the terms of discussion of population questions, but not until the later part of the eighteenth century was there any marked shift in the general attitude favouring large and increasing population. The mercantilist and cameralist schools of political economy, which flourished in Europe during much of the seventeenth and the eighteenth century, emphasized the economic, political and military advantages of large and growing population and favoured various measures to stimulate population growth. These writers were concerned primarily with the ways and means of increasing the wealth and power of the State. Their aim was not to promote per capita income but to increase the aggregate national income which was viewed as a sources of revenue for the State.

During the last half of the eighteenth century, a number of writers on economic and social questions rejected the mercantilist doctrine and the view that population growth was advantageous and should be actively encouraged by the State. Some writers, specially in England, France and Italy, emphasised the dependence of population upon means of subsistence. They opposed arrangement for poor relief on the ground that it might undermine frugality, make labour immobile, depress productivity and thus increase the pressure of number on means of subsistence. These arguments were turned against such advocates of social reform as Godwin and Condorect, in an effort to show that any benefits from reform would be cancelled by a consequent increase of populations.

At the close of eighteenth century, Thomas Malthus, an English economist, noted this tendency for populations, including human population to increase rapidly. In 1798, he published his famous work, Essay on the principal of population, in which he put forth the idea that populations tend to increase faster than their means of subsistence. In general, he felt that populations tended to increase geometrically or exponentially, whereas their food supplies and means of subsistence tended to increase only arithmetically. A geometric increase is a series of numbers having a common ratio, such as 2...4...8...16...32...64 in which each succeeding number is twice the former. An arithmetic increase is a series of number having a common difference, such as 2...4...6...8...10...12, in which each number differs from the other by 2. Thus, Malthus thought that populations constantly tended to outstrip their food supplies and were then decimated by poverty, starvation, disease, warfare, or other catastrophes. Malthus was primarily concerned with human populations, and he felt that moral restraint was the solution to human population pressures.

Malthus's theory is thus based on two postulates and one assumption. His postulates are that (i) food is necessary for the existence of man, and (ii) that passion between sexes is necessary, and will remain nearly in its present form. The assumption is that the production of food increases in arithmetical progression while the population increases in geometrical progression. Thus the power of population is indefinitely greater than the power of the earth to produce subsistence for men. Efforts must, therefore, be made to keep the population from growing beyond the means of subsistence through some powerful checks, else it will lead to "vice and misery."

Malthus talked of two kinds of checks to population positive and preventive. He termed preventive check as "prudence" and included in it postponement of marriage and restraint on reproduction. Positive checks he termed as "natural" as "they arise form the situation itself" and included in it wars, pestilence, epidemics, diseases, famines, natural calamities and the like.

Malthus was highly praised and also bitterly criticised for his views. His Essay aroused a storm of controversy which long out-lived Malthus himself, and which made both his followers and his opponents conscious of the need for adequate information on population trends and their influence on social and economic conditions. Thus Malthus was indirectly responsible for developing population censuses a vital statistics. Malthus has been criticised for his postulates, his assumptions and his conclusions. While it is not to be disputed that food is necessary for man, but so is water clothes, shelter, and such other prime necessities of life. There is enough historical evidence to indicate that the output of food and of other necessities has increased faster than population, and has been brought about without any distinct symptoms of increasing "misery and vice", but rather of their diminution. With improvement in techniques of production increasing returns are being obtained from land and from the production of prime necessities of life.

Malthus has proved a false prophet. While he postulated great miseries on account of unprecedented growth of population, it is found that birth rate in most of the advanced countries of the world has declined, and that the rapid growth of population in under-developed countries is basically due to a rapid fall in death rate and not on account, as Malthus feared, of an increase in birth rate.

Marx rejected the Malthusion theory of population. He held that there is no universal law of population, and that the source of "over-population" was not to be found in man's biological power of reproduction, but in prevailing capitalistic mode of production. Over population arose because capital accumulated less rapidly than did the supply of labouring population was not only a necessary consequence of capita-listic accumulation, but also a necessary condition for the existence and continuation of the capitalistic form of economic organisation.

The realisation that Malthus has over-generalised a particular case lead to a re-thinking of the population question. Writers at the beginning of the present century began thinking that population growth is not always undesirable. This led to the development of the optimum theory of population which is associated with the name of Professor Cannan and others.

The theory says that given the natural resources and the technique of production, that population, Cannan envisaged a point of maximum return for all industries taken together, that is the population which will maximise productivity. He also indicated that the optimum size of the population changes as circumstances change and as new techniques of production are introduced.

Effort to precisely define the "optimum" led to the refinement of the concept, but at the same time to the theory being criticised as of little practical value. It is considered highly artificial to select "average real income "as the soletest of the optimum. In fact there can be an optimum size of the population from ecological, political and other points of view. Again, the optimum size is subject to frequent changes on account of changes in techniques of production.

The transition theory, development in the 30's of third century and associated with names of Warmn S. Thompson and Frank W. Notestein, explains the relationship between population with and economic development. It says that in developing countries, which are characterised by heavy pressure of population, low productivity heavy dependence on agriculture, rudimentary techniques of production, under-developing means of transport, and poor sanitary conditions, birth and death rate high. Death rates are high because of poor diet, primitive sanitation, and the absence of preventive and curative medical facilities. Birth rates are high because of social beliefs and customs which encourage large families and which group up if a high death-rate community is to continue its existence. The birth rate around 40 per one thousand person and the death rate around 35 so that the population does not grow at a fast rate.

With economic progress the death rate begins to decline. This is because of improved means of transport, better sewage disposal and improvement in drinking water facilities. But the birth rate stays high so that the difference population tend to grow at the rate of 20-30 per thousand population per year. Because of the rapid rate at which the population grows, this period is also known as that of "population explosion".

One of the features of economic development is typically increasing urbanisation and in an urban setting children are usually more of the burden and less of an asset. The processed economic change also weakens the force of traditional customs and beliefs. Females are being to realize that if burdened with a large family they are unlikely to play their due role in society. Consequently, the idea of large family yields place to the small-family-death and the birth rate declines from the high 40 to about 17 per one thousand population. The death rate is also low, about 8 per one thousand, so that the population just maintains itself.

The three stages described above are also called the stages of slow population growth, rapid population growth and of stable or declining population growth. The industrially advanced countries of the world have passed through the first-two stages and are current in third stage. Developing countries of Asia, Africa and Latin America are either in the first stage or entering the second stage.

The sequence of events described by the theory can be traced in every region when the economy has evolved from an agrarian to an industrial market oriented economy. But it is not specific to quantity if the degree of decline of the vital rates. The theory, however, contains one significant generalisation, namely, the decline in birth rate occur after a substantial time-lag in comparing with the decline in death rate, and that during this lag population increases very rapidly. For instance, the "area of European settlement" increased its population six fold during the period 1750 and 1950. The population more than doubled in the century from 1750 to 1850 and nearly tripled in the period 1850 to 1950.

The theory is of considerable significance to under developed countires of Asia, Africa and Latin America. Their birth rate is high and the field of public health, it has been possible for the death rate to be substantially reduced with marked changes in the economy or in the birth rate., Consequently, their population is growing at a rate which doubles itself in twenty to twenty-five years. This is tending to retard economic progress. There is therefore an urgent need for bringing about a substantial decline in birth rates if economic development is to become a continuing process.

Logistic growth

The first major scientific challenge to Malthusian doctrine as a pattern of population growth appeared in the 1830's in the work of Pierre Verhulst. In 1839 Verhulst proposed that population normally grow in a much more orderly fashion than that proposed by Malthus, describing in their growth a curve of S-shaped proportion. This became known as the Logistic Theory of population growth. The logistic theory asserted that population have a slow initial growth rate, which increases exponentially unitl it reaches a maximum, and then becomes progressively less as the population approaches an upper limit of its growth. The upper limit is approached gradually and in an orderly, predictable manner. The resulting curve is the familiar S-shaped of population growth.

It should be noted that the logistic curve and the Malthusian or irrupting curve do not differ in the early stages of population growth—both show a slow start followed by a period of exponential or geometric growth but they do differ fundamentally in the upper or controlling stages of growth. The Malthusian curve is characterized by an erratic, often catastrophic, pattern of limiting growth, whereas the logistic curve characterized by a smooth, orderly and gradual pattern.

Following the work of Verhulst, the logistic theory lay dormant unto it was independently derived and popularized by Raymond Pearl in the 1920's. Pearl applied the logistic curve to the population growth of yeast, Drosophila and man. This ushered forth a burst of activity resulting in the application of the logistic curve to the population growth of protozoa, water fleas, pond snails, thrips, ants, bees and other organisms by many investigators.

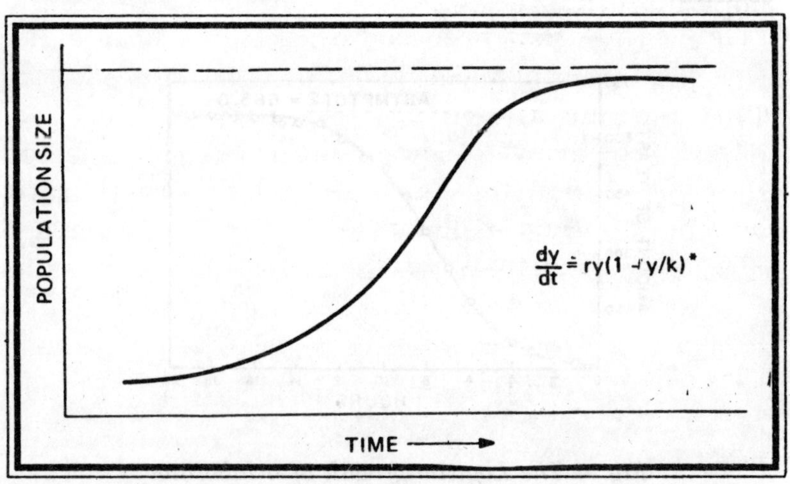

Fig.4 Population growth pattern typical of logistic or S-shaped growth

With this wealth supporting evidence, the logistic thoery attained wide acceptance. It was proclaimed as a law of population growth by some biologists and was used to predict future population levels of experimental and natural population. Pearl's investigation led him to conclude (1930): "It has been shown in what has preceded that populations of living thing `from the simplest' represented by yeast, to the highest, represented by man, grow in accordance with the logistic curve). One can now feel more certain that this curve is a first and tolerable close approximation to a real law of growth for human populations.... We can, for example, upon a more adequate scientific basis mere than guess-work, predict future population, or estimate past populations, outside the range of known census counts."

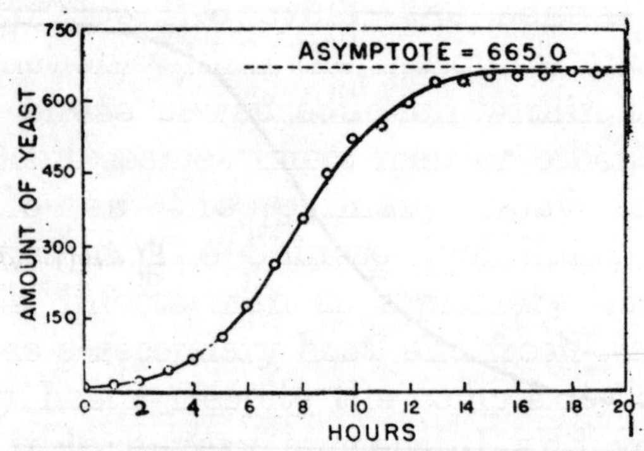

Fig. 4 The Logistic growth of a laboratory population of yearst cells.

That some biologist accepted Pearl's interpretation rather freely is indicated by statements of Clarke (1954): "Population of a wide variety of organisms, ranging from bacteria to whales, have been found to follow the logistic curve in the growth from.... The growth of man's population follows a similar pattern whether examined in individual regions or in the world as a whole. "Clarke presented a graph of population growth in the United States fitted with a logistic curve, and observed an upper symptote of 184 million in year 2100 A.D.

Many other biologists and mathematicians, however, severely criticized the significance of the logistic theory. In fact, the theory met stern opposition since its first expression could be made to fit a wide variety of curves, often of very different nature. Gray (1929), Hongben (1931), and Wilson and Puffer (1933) registered doubt as to the universal validity of ligistic theory and commented on its inadequacies as a description. Feller (1940) pointed out that the actual fit of the logistic curve to much of the published data was poor and better agreement could be obtained with other formulas. Andrewartha and Birch (1954) and sang (1950) accurately pointed to limitations of the logistic equation. Sang (1950) in careful reexamination of population growth in Drosophila, emphasized that, "The data we have summarized show that only in very exceptional circumstances would logistic growth occur in a Drosophila culture... The ecological situation is too complex to be adequately described as the Pear-Verhulst law, "Sang continued to discuss general aspect of the logistic theory by stating, "This acceptance of a plausible formula, in spite of its inaccuracy, may be justified; provided this attitude does not inhibit future research, particularly in to fundamental conception. In the case reviewed, it seems that wide acceptance of the logistic law has led to just this kind of inhibition of further work, and that many interesting ecological and physiological processes have been ignored as a result.

The study of vertebrate population in both natural and confined circumstances has produced some population growth curves deviating considerably for logistic growth and tending to ward errupting or Malthusian growth. The sheep population of southern Australia showeed a pattern of liogistic-like growth from 1840 to 1890, but its upper level was reached abruptly and was followed by substantial mortality. The deer of Kaibab National Forest in Arizona grew from an estimated population of 4,000 animals in 1918 after a period of extensive predator control to an estimated population of 1,00,000 in 1924 but in the winter of 1924, they died by the thousands after the population had destroyed its food supply. Their growth and decline described a classic Malthusian curve. The pheasant population of Protection Island, Washington, showed a phenomenal increase from 8 birds on the 397 acre island in 1937 to nearly 2,000 birds by 1942. In one year the population showed an increase of 3000 percent. Unfortunately the field research on this population was terminated before natural control occurred, but the population seemed to be describing a typical irrupting population curve.

Several studies of seminatural populations of wild house mice have also shown irrupting population curves. Seminatural populations have been maintained in confined, but free-ranging conditions with a natural habit for this species, except for the element of confinement. Various factors such as space, food supply, resting cover and the structure of the physical environment have been experimentally controlled to elucidate their roles in population growth and limitation Work of this type at the University of Wiconsin and the Institute of Ecology in Warsaw Poland, has shown that population growth in *house mice* is highly variable, and often dependent upon patterns of sicial behaviour within the population. For example, populations in identical environments showed widely variable patterns of population growth. The variability was related to social behaviour within the population in terms of aggressive behavior, dominance hierarchies, sexual behaviour and parental care. All populations become controlled even though abundant food and nesting space was still available when aggressive behavior increased to an abnormal degree, when the nesting territories of females were no longer properly maintained, and when parental care of the nestlings become aberrant. Infant mortality increased through nest desertion and cannibalism. The densities at which these behavioral pathologies occurred were highly variable between populations, and they were function of the crowding tolerance and behavioral stability of individuals. This complicated interplay of ecology and social behavior was not adequately accounted for by the logistic theory and the resulting population curves were totally individualistic and unpredictable.

A fairly complete evaluation of logistic theory has been presented by Andrewartha and Birch.

They have analyzed the inherent assumptions of the logistic equation and have reviewed many studies in the light of these assumptions. The analysis has led them to conclude that the logistic curve provides an inperfect, yet useful, description of the population growth of organisms with simple life histories (such as yeast and Paramecium); but for animals with complex life histories (such as insects and vertebrates) the population growth usually does not conform closely to the logistic curve except for small parts of the data.

The concluding attitude of Andrewartha and Birch is well experessed in the following. "despite its theoretical limitations, the logistc curve remains a useful tool for the ecologist. Because of its limitations, too much reliance should not be placed on it in particular cases until it has been verified empirically for each case. "Hence, it appears fallacious to utilize the logistic equation of a prognostic purpose in any population without experimental precedence.

The evidence is clear, therefore, to support the early contention of Wilson and Puffer (1933) that the logistic formula should not be considered a law of population growth to such an extent that it permits extrapolation of the curve of forecasting purposes or the interpretation that the constants of the equation are the constants for nature. Rather, it does provide a convenient description of growth in certain well-studied populations.

The major question in human terms is, of course, what pattern of population growth characterizes man? From the early seventeenth century to the present time, the world's population has displayed exponential growth. There seems to be widespread faith that human populations shall ultimately reveal a logistic pattern, but certainly all attempts to predict human population levels by means of the logistic model have been very far from the mark. Pearl predicted a world population of 2.6 million by the year 2100. This population level was exceeded many years ago, and economic planning based on Pearl's prediction would indeed have been disastrous. Although we continue to hope that human population throughout the world will achieve a pattern of graduallogistic balance through orderly and intentional process, there is no sound scientific evidence that this will in fact occur. The possible of catastrophic mortality through war, disease and starvation are still very much with us. So also are other patterns of mortality which are not necessarily catastrophic in their total effect, but are clearly related to density, crowding and modern population pressures. In this category are automobile accident mortalities, which are responsible for 50,000 deaths per year in the United States alone, various stress-related diseases, including coronary artery disease and high blood pressure, and various pollution-related diseases including emphysema and chronic bronchitis. If deaths attributable to these causes continue to show present trends, these mortality factors will begin to play a more significant role in population regulation, especially in technologically advanced countries.

Population Fluctuations

Different patterns of population growth may be exhibited by populations recovering from major depletions, or by populations invading new inhabitants. Since most populations are already established, however, and are not growing de novo, they are instead showing varying degrees of fluctuations. Our familiar concept of the balance of nature implies stability but the fact is that most animal populations under go continual change. Natural populations often exhibit a dynamic resiliency, rising and falling in response to many factors. In one sense, a pattern of population fluctuation such as that normally exhibited by most species, may be considered continuous series of growth & decline sequeuces. Thus study of population fluctuation becomes closely allied with the study of population growth and natural control.

Seasonal fluctuations

At the outset it is convenient to separate population fluctuations which are seasonal (i.e., obviously related to seasonal weather), from those which are nonseasonal latitudes, most animal pupulations have breeding seasons so that population growth typically occurs in the spring and summer seasons. Most arthropods and vertebrates begin producing young in the spring and summer seasons, so that these seasons are characterized by population growth, and they cease the production of young in laten autumn and winter.

In aquatic ecosystems, many populations also show marked seasonal fluctuations. Both phytoplankton (miscoroscopic algae), and zooplankton (protozoa rotifiers, small crustacea, etc.) usually show spring and fall increases in population. These sharp increases, often 10 to 20 fold, are known as "pulses". They are sometimes correlated with temperature changes or with turnovers in the water state which recirculate nutrients.

In the tropical regions of the world, where there are not sharply defined seasons on a temperature basis, reproductive seasonality still occurs in many plants and animals, and it is often related to the cycle of wet and dry seasons. Many tropical insects, for example, have sharp peaks of abundance related to the monsoon seasons. Even vertebrate animals, including primates, have been found in nature to have definite periods of breeding and birth seasons, often correlated with the monsoons.

In both tropic and temperate zones an important principle seems to be that the young appear at the most favourable time of the year in term of food and climate. Thus young deer and antelope are born when insect food is most readily available. These are exceptions to this general principle; for example, young rhesus monkeys are born in the midst of the hot dry season in northern India, when temperatures are excessively high (often over 100 degree F), water is extremely scarce, and plant growth is virtually nil. In this case, however, the infant feeds exclusively on the mother's milk for two or three months until the monsoon season starts. It is possible that natural selection has acted in such a way as to place breeding, conception and the first trimester of pregnancy at the most favorable time of the year, namely, the immediate postmonsoon month when food is most abundant. In other words, the events of conception and early embryonic growth may have been more critical in the life cycle of the rhesus monkey in terms of evironmental influences than the period of early infancy which is well protected by the mother and the social group. This is speculation and not established fact at this time. It also fits with the observation, however, that the monsoon season with its luxuriant growth again arrives when the infant is two or three months old and is relying less on maternal milk and starts taking its own food.

Population fluctuations which are relatively independent of seasons are of two general types: (1) random, or (2) cyclic. Cyclic fluctuations are those which have a definite periodicity, or rhythmicity; that is, the population reaches a peak at fairly regular intervals. In vertebrate populations, certain species reach population peaks every 4 years, while other have a 10-year cycle. These will be discussed later as specialized cases of more generalized random fluctuations.

Ramdom fluctuations

Ramdom fluctuations may be minor perturbations of fairly stable population, producting relatively flat curves, or they may be major changes in abundance, producing erratic unstable curves.

Examples of stable populations are increasingly difficult to find in the modern world. They were probably characteristic of many organisms in undisturbed ecosystems; that is, ecosystems in balance. They were also probably characteristic of complex systems, such as forests and particularly tropical forests where great species diversity produced a complicated web of natural check and balances on each species. Within such a system most vertebrate populations were probably stable and exhibited only their typical seasonal fluctuations.

Probably some of the best modern examples of stable populations may be found among the birds and larger mammals. In birds where considerable species diversity occurs and fairly extensive food resources are available, considerable stability in population size may be present. John Gibb (1961) reviewed a number of bird population studies several years ago and noted: "Notwithstanding the considerable annual fluctuation is bird populations that have been recorded in almost every species investigated, it is their comparative stability over long periods that is their most remarkable attribute. "Thus, although wide variations is number occur form year to year in many bird population, these population often show a tendency to return to typical levels.

An example of a relatively stable vertebrate population is afforded by a census study of rhesus monkey populations (Macaca mulatta) in northern India. With complete protection, good health and abundant food supplies, rhesus populations can increase in experimental colonies at the rate of 15 per cent per year. But in India, where monkey experience limited food supplies, varying degrees of protection from the human population, and a considerable number of infections diseases, populations do not show this pattern of increase.

In general, throughout India as in most of the world, primate population are declining due to habitat deterioration (cutting of forest, overgrazing of savannah lands, etc.) human competition (where native people shoot monkeys for food), and high rates of trapping for commercial trade. As an example of the latter, in the late 1950's India exported more than 100,000 monkeys per year for use in biomedical research and pharmaceutical production, though the current figure is only about onehalf of this. These monkeys were essential in the development of polio vaccine, measeles vaccine, and many types of medical and psychological research.

The long term population trend of many animals, especially wild vertebrate animals, is down ward. Since 1600 A.D., 120 species of birds and mammals have become extinct, a number several times greater than the natural rate of extinction. At the present time, approximately one vertebrate animal become extinct on the face of the earth every year, and within the next 30 to 50 years, 100 more species will probably be lost. The International Union of the Conservation of Nature periodically publishes a list of rare and endangered species (the publication is known as the Red Data Book), and it now lists nearly 300 species of birds and 275 species of mammals as endangered. The peregrine falcon (Falco peregrinus), ospery (Pandion haliaetus), and bald eagle (Haliaectus leuocephalus) are presently among the vanishing animals of North America. Others have come close to extinction, but were saved by intensive conservation movement at the last moment.

Throughout the world, the basic causes of extinction are habitat deterioration, poaching, poisoning, and direct or indirect competition with man. From the ecological standpoint, some extinction is an inevitable evolutionary process, but when it becomes excessive as in the last century, it is a serious disruption to biotic communities and ecosystems. Each extinction lessens species diversity, and thereby reduces ecosystem stability. Each estinction also represents the irreplaceable loss of unique biological material.

It should be pointed out of course, that some vertebrate animals have increased drastically within the last century, but these are usually domestic animals such as dogs, cats, cattle, goats and so forth, or wild animals that have learned to become commensal with man; that is, animals which have successfully adapted and even exploited the human environment. This includes the domestic rats and mice such as the Norway rat, the house mouse the Asian bandicoot rat (Bandicota bengalensis),the Asian house shrew (Suncus murina) to starling, the house sparrow and the pigeon (Columba livea.) Even the herring gull (Larus argentatus) is adapting to man's urban environment successfully by feeding on garbage dumps, and gull population on both United States coasts have increased in recent years.

Apart from those species which seem to be headed towards a permanent decline and eventual extinction, and those which thrive on man-made environments, the fact remains that most animal population fluctuate substantially from year to year.

It is often a matter of common knowledge among farmers and sportsmen that "this is a good year for pheasants,"or "there were rabbits all over the place last year, but not so many this year," or "this is the world year for mosquitoes we've ever had," and so forth. These are all popular expressions of population fluctuations. Scientifically, these fluctuations are not often recorded in a systematic and continuous fashion, but some data do exist to document the types of fluctuations which are common in animal populations.

In trying to manage animal populations, we tend to do the most obvious thing, which would logically seem to produce results, and often does, but in the long run, may be quite detrimental to the total ecological balance of a community. Thus, in controlling insect populations, we use residual poisons such as DDT, but are now discovering after some 30 years, that this has long term side effects which are quite dangerous, and we are also dicovering that many insects have become resistant to it in any case. In controlling the population levels and general health of their prey species.

In enhancing the abundance of desirable species, we have often poured money into artificial breeding and restocking programes of animals such as pheasant, wild turkeys and trout only to find that in the meantime, the habitat has so deteriorated through pollution that the transplants have little or no change of success, and the recovery rate per transplant is almost nil. This is not intended as a blanket condemnation of all of our control and management programs, but by and large the balance sheet is not favourable, mainly because we have based our management on trial and error rather than on sound basic knowledge of the ecological factors involved in population growth and regulation.

Population cycles

The most diamatic population fluctuations are those which are cyclic: that is, in which the population reaches peak numbers at fairly regular intervals. Some animal populations, such as those of the snowshoe hare (Lepus americana) have periodicity of abundance of 9 to 10 years.

Other animal populations have a cyclical periodicity of 3 to 4 years. These include the Norway lemming of Scandinavia (Lemmus lemmus), the field mouse (Microtus agrestis) of Europe, and some of the predators of these two notably the colored fox (Vulpes fulva) and the snowy owl (Nyctea scandiaca). Not all populations of these animals always fluctuate cyclically. When they appear to do so, sophisticated statistics may be required for proof of real cyclic periodicity.

These animal population cycles have been intriguing and puzzling to biologists for many years. Considerable research has been centered around trying to understand the cause of cycles, and numerous theories have been proposed to account for them. The final answers are still not clear, though many biological phenomena have been discovered and analyzed in this search for understanding.

In general, two types of factors have been considered as the basic causes of animal population cycles:(1) extrinsic factors; that is, those outside of the population itself, such as climate and weather, cosmic events competition between species, predator-prey relationship's and food supply; or (2) intrinsic factors; that is those within the animals as population increases occur and they become crowded.

Several of these factors can be dismissed rather quickly, since extenive research has failed to show any clear relationship. For example climatic and meteorological changes have not been satisfactorily correlated with regular long-term cycles of population change in any animal. Sometimes population peaks coincide with years of great rainfall, or some other notable aspect of weather, but these occurrences are by no means consistent.

At one time, sunspot cycles were considered to be correlated with population cycles. Sunspot maixma have occurred every 10 to 11 years, and they were correlated with peak population of hares and lynx in the late eighteenth and early ninteenthe century, but in the late eighteeth and early ninteenth century, but in the last 100 years, have been entirely out of phase.

Changes of populations of predators such as the lynx, fox and sowy owl are clearly correlated with cycles of their prey. But they cannot be shown to cause the prey cycles, for prey cycles often occur in areas devoid of predators. For example snowshoe hare populations have cycles in areas where no lynx are found.

There has been some attention given to disease and parastism as the cause of long-term cycles. Twenty years ago there was interest in hypoglycemic shock in snowshoe hares. Animals at peak periods of abundance seemed to have low blood sugar levels and go into states of shock and death. This was interpreted as the alarm reaction of Selye's general adaptions syndrome. There has also been considerable work on tuberculosis and toxoplasmosis in wild voles and although high disease rates have occasionally been asociated with die-offs of peak population, these associations have not been consistent. Many rodent declines have occourred without evidence of an infectious disease as the cause. Most ecologists have not been well trained in pathology, bacteriology and virology, not have scientists in these disciplines extended their work satisfactorily to population ecology.

Food supply has often been considered inportant in the decline of animal populations. Lack (1954) proposed that food is the main limiting factor in bird populations as it is for deer population in North America, Most field studies of rodents have demonstrated however, that even at peak periods of abundance ample food is present. Chitty (1960) studied grass during and after high vole plagues and found ample food. There are exceptions; for instance, during lemming peaks food becomes severely depleted and this is one of the factors that is though to start lemming migrations. Pitelka (1958) felt that insufficient attention has been paaid to qualitative study of food. The estrogents and steroid in growing plants, particularly grasses and legumes, are now being studied. It has been observed in the Orients, for example, that upsurges of rodent populations are often timed with the flowering and sprouting of bamboo. Then there is not only increased supply, but the young growing plants are more nutritive and estrogens are increased. The estrogens have direct influence on fertility and fecundity of the animals feeding on them.

3 Population Environment and Resources

Status of environment vis-a-vis population explosion

India is the second most population country in the world. According to the 1981 census the population of the country was 685 million, which crossed the 800 million mark in 1988. Every year an additional 17million babies are born. At the current rate the population will grow to nine billion by the turn of the century and this number will double by the year 2035. In all probability India will overtake China as the most populous country on the earth in the next four decades.

Today India accounts for 15 percent of the world population while its land area constitutes only 2.4 per cent. The per capita availability of land in the country is 0.48 hectares as against 4.14 hectares in the USA and 8.43 hectares in the USSR. The main-land ration in relation to arable land is on 0.27 hectares and it is likely to reduce further in the coming years. Already India is twice as densely populated as China, putting heavy pressure on the environment, resources infrastructure and basic services. Providing basic human need for such a large population are continue to remain a major task. The needs of the rapidly growing population are likely to overtake the ability of the nation to provide essential service like health care, education, employment opportunities, housing etc. There is chronic shortage of safe drinking water both in rural and urban areas, about 20 per cent of the urban and 50 percent of the rural population is still to be provided with safe drinking water.

Urbanisation, a phenomenon closely related with burgeoning population, has swallowed up approximately 1.5 million hectares of agricultural land in the past 30 years. In addition 1.3 million hectares of forest was lost each year during 1975-82. The shortage of housing is an ever growing problem. Over one-fifth of the urban population lives in slums. In Bombay, Delhi and Culcutta about 3—40 per cent of the population resides in slums. Many of the problems experienced in accommodating a growing family in a one-room house on a small plot ae analogous to those posed by expanding population. The size of the earth is fixed and its resources are strictly finite. Demands upon natural resources expand rapidly while their per capita availability decreases progressively, damaging the natural resource base.

The consequences of environmental degradation and resource scarcity hit the poor most severely. To stay alive these people destroy the very resources they will need tomorrow. The resultant damage to the environment only depend their poverty. The vivious circle of poverty and environmental destruction is at work. The 'scissors effect' of poverty and increasing population slices away their ability to sustain human life. The victims of poverty destroy forests for fuel-wood-, food, water and fodder and the growing population forces them to farm marginal land at non-sustainable levels. The excessive resource exploitation combined with a poor understanding of the interrelationships between man and environment has thus led to ecological crisis. Soil erosion and land degradation, deforestation, the fuelwood shortage, problems of water management, excessive population pressure on land and other environment-degrading trends inhibit the pace of economic development.

The mounting problems of pollution consequent upon unimaginative interference of human beings with nature have been adversely affecting the quality of life. Pollutants may be regarded as resources at the wrong place, but as such they represent a continuous drain on resources, apart from their disruptive or degrading impact on air, soil and water. However, the harsh reality of the environmental crisis-shinking of forests, increasing desertification, degradation of critical resources, loss of agricultural land, salanisation, alkalisation and waterlogging, acidification of the environment and release of hazardous waste has created environmental awareness among planners and policy makers. Building environmental concerns into development is now regarded as making efforts for sustained life and for avoiding the imminent death trap.

Sustainable development

The concept of sustainability has emerged as a key issue in development-planning very recently. The Stockholm Conference on the Human Environment 1972 and the International Conference on Population held in 1948 at Mexico City reflected concern for sustainable development. The International planned Parenthood Federation and the international Union for Conservation of Nature ad Natural Resources have also stressed this approach to development. The recent report or the World Commission on Environment and Development, headed by the Norwegian Prime Minister Mrs. Brundtland has used it as a key concept.

The need for sustainable development presupposes that the present development is not sustainable, and hence it is urged to opt for a new approach to development.

There is need to integrate population, environment and natural resource policies into national development strategies so as to ensure environmentally sound sustainable development. The major emphasis of this approach is on meeting the basic needs of the people and improving their quality of life without adversely affecting the viability of the environment. It requires development strategies which anticipate environmental problems and take precautionary measures to avoid the resultant problems.

However, the goal of sustainable development is not likely to be attained unless the implications off interrelationships among population, environment, resources and development are adequately understood and appreciated by the people of the country. It is urgently required to removed the insularity of perception of growing degradation of environment and critical resources in the context of rapid population growth and the process of development. This is possible when a proper understanding of environmental problems and their possible solutions is developed. An attempt, therefore, is being made in the following pages to discus major environmental problems such as deforestation, soil erosion, flooding, excessive ground water exploitation, threat to wide-life, use of chemicals and pesticides, unimaginative mining water, ocean and air pollution, acidification, green house effect and ozone depletion. The efforts to improve the quality of environment and the issue of conservation and utilization of natural resources have also been delineated.

Deforestation

Forests represent a well organised and highly evolved community of plants and animals. They provide several products of daily use such as food, timber, fire-wood, wood pulp, forage and fibre, apart from being a vast store house of medicinal plants which are yet to be fully explored and exploited. They are potent sources of many industrial raw materials. The greatest significance of forests, however, lies in their critical role in maintaining ecological processes and life support systems.

According to official records 23 per cent of the land in India is classified as forests. The National Forest Policy of 1952 recommended that 33 per cent of the land area of the country should be under forests. Contrary to this guideline, however, forests have been under increasing assault since independence. It has been estimated that 1.3 million hectares of forests are lost every year. Land under forests shrunk from 46.42 million hectares in 1972-75 to 33.77 million hectares in 1980-82. At present not more than 10 to 12 per cent of the land is estimated to be under forest cover excessive exploitation of forests and overgrazing by cattle have seriously decimated our forest resource. The denudation of the Himalayan and other hilly area had led to soil erosion which affects river water quality, apart from inducing rapid siltation of dams and reservoirs. Degradation of forests leads to the destruction of wild life habitats. Over a hundred species of wild animals need immediate protection, as their populations have swindled to dangerously low levels. Moreover, many plants have suffered from deforestation and destruction. In a recent list prepared by the Botanical Survey of india there are 135 species of plants that need immediate care for their continued survival.

Deforestation also greatly increased the workload of local communities. Women and children, in particular, are forced to bear the burden of collecting fuel, water and food. A study in Almora reveals that because of indiscriminate deforestation the agricultural production, which was once sufficient, now sufficient, now feeds that villagers only for seven months in a year, as soil productivity has diminished and population has grown. Fire-woods and water have to be hauled from longer distançes, because forests have shrunk and the springs in the neighborhood, once abounding in sparkling fresh water, have dried up. Pre-occupation with fire wood collection and hauling of drinking water leaves little time for the villagers to address themselves to other activities essential for socio-economic development improvement in their quality of life

Soil erosion

Soil is the essential medium for the growth of plants. Management and improvement of soil fertility is vital for agricultural production and economic prosperity. But the pressure of the growing human and cattle populations has seriously affected the soil resources. The total cultivable land area in India is about 304 million hectares. According to an estimate made by the Ministry of Agriculture in march 1980, as much as 175 million hectares of this land area is suffering from environmental degradation. Deforestation, overgrazing, unscientific agricultural practices and desertification have induced soil erosion.

In Rajasthan, where only 20 per cent of the land is suitable for rainfed cropping, the mounting population pressure has doubled the area under cultivation from 30 per cent in 1951 to 60 per cent in 1971. This has happened mainly at the expense of grazing land necessary for pastoral agriculture which is the main occupation of a large section of the population in the state. With the population density already twenty times that of arid lands elsewhere in the world, the pressure of the growing population has led to various kinds of environmental implications. More land being brought under cultivation, a decrease in grazing land, deforestation caused by rising demand for fuel and fodder, mounting pressure on land for house construction and other related developments have increased the desertification of western Rajasthan. This problem has been aggravated by wind and water erosion, water-logging, saline and alkali soils, primarily because of over-straining of the land resources.

Soil degradation has serious economic and ecological implications for a country like india which has a prodiminently agricultural economy. For example, nutrient losses caused on account of NPK alone represents a loss of Rs. 700 crores per annum. Moreover, stream bank erosion and shifting of river courses through silt deposition by flood-prone systems affect the land use pattern. Soil erosion increases the silt load in a river system affecting aquatic productivity diversely and results in speedier siltation of dams and reservoirs. Siltation of dams reduced their effective life span, a factor which has serious economic and ecological implications.

The practice of cultivation, adopted in hilly areas covered with forest, has been a major cause of soil degradation. It is popularly known as the *Jhum* cultivation. It involves clearing of the forest by burning and using the cleared area for cultication. But on such fields cultivation is possible only for 3 to 4 years, after which the area is abandoned, as the soil fertility goes done. Thereafter a new forest area is cleared for cultivation. The abandoned area is used for regenerating the forest so that soil fertility is restored. In the past the cycle of this process used to take considerably longer duration. Since the population of the *Jhum* cultivator was small, it took about 600 to 1000 years of more to return to the same land for cultivation. But now a days the duration of the *Jhum* cycle has been drastically

reduced, mainly because of the needs of the rapidly growing population on those areas. Currently, only after every 4 to 10 years the same land is brought again under the *Jhúm* cultivation. The reduced *Jhum* cycle is inadequate to recuperate the soil fertility. The continuation of the *jhum* cultivation, therefore, is increasingly promoting land degradation.

Flooding

On account of deforestation, tampering with nature, uncontrolled grazing in the catchment areas and soil erosion, floods have become a recurring phenomenon in many parts of the country. According to the report of the National Commission on Floods the total area affected by annual; floods had doubled since independence. While in the 1950s and 1960s three-fourths of all flood damage took place in five states, since the mid-seventies half the damage has been occurring outside the traditional flood zones. Loss of human lives and livestock as well as economic losses and damages to property are escalating steadily.

The average economic loss due to floods during 1971-78 was nearly Rs. 1000 crore annually.

In the absence of proper land-use planning, floods have become increasingly devastating over the years. Moreover, the pressure of population growth force people to encroach upon flood plains. The disastrous impact of floods magnifies as the size of the population inhabiting flood plains and river banks increases.

Excessive ground water exploitation

Ground water or aquifer is another major pool of fresh water that has been exploited by mankind from time immemorial. Ground water is periodically recharged by the rain water that seeps through the soil. It represents an important decentralized source of water supply which is available round the year. The total annual exploitable potential of ground water in the country is estimated at 42.3 m ha m (million hectare metre) of which only 10 m ha m is being exploited at present.

Ground water exploitation for agriculture, industry and human consumption is rapidly increasing in many parts of the country to meet the demand of the growing population. Large scale exploitation of ground water through dug wells and tube wells has created severe problems in many parts of the country. In many areas, ground water withdrawals have far exceeded the reaharging capacity of the aquifer, resulting in lowering of the water level and drying of wells. Intensively cropped one has undertake deep drilling. This calls for heavy expenditure, which is generally beyond the means of the average cultivators. This has resulted in chronic shortages of drinking water in many parts of Gujarat and Maharashtra. Over-withdrawal of ground water in many coastal areas has promoted salt water or sea water intrusion, which has made the ground water unfit for drinking and irrigation. The use of ground water needs to be strictly regulated to prevent its population and over-exploitation.

Threat to wild life

Flora and fauna are priceless fights of nature. They provide the essential underpinnings for cultural, industrial and economic development of a country. Nature has been very generous to india in providing a rich variety of flora and fauna which constitute its wildlife. The richness of Indian wildlife can easily compare with that of any other country of the world. More than 1200 species of birds and 500 species of mammals exist in the indian region and include such animals as the elephant, the gigantic himalayan sheep, the Indian bison or guar, deer, cheeta, the four-horned antelope, the black-buck, the dancing deer or thamin, the one-horned rhinoceros, the lion and the tiger. It is however pertinent to note that populations of wildlife species are rapidly dwindling and many species,e.g. tiger and lion, once present in large numbers, are endangered today.

Rapid increase in human and bovine populations has promoted large-scale habitat destruction by bringing more land under the plough and implementing developmental projects. This eventually has adverse impact on wildlife. Today-, the future of wild animals is, in general, alarming. Many endangered species are fighting a loosing a battle for survival. The worst victims, no doubt, are the fur-bearing mammals, birds with ornamental feathers and reptiles. Elephants are hunted for ivory and the rhinoceros is prized for its horn. About 350 species constitute the mammalian fauna of India, of which 81 are endangered. Examples of wildlife extinction in recent times are that of the Indian cheeta, the one-horned rhino and the Sikkim stag, and among the birds, the mountain quail, and probably among the timed species the Jerdon's courser. Over one hundred species of wild animal need immediate protection as their populations have swindled to dangerously low levels.

Similarly, many plant species have suffered from the onslaught of human activities. Wild plants and animals are sources of many industrial raw materials in addition to providing a variety of other goods and services. It will be great tragedy, if wildlife is allowed to suffer from thoughtless destruction of their habitat by over exploitation, poaching or ignorance.

Use of chemicals and pesticides

Fertilizers

The rapid pace of population growth demands increase in food production. Since independence, Indian has tripped its cereal production by adopting modern means of agriculture. Chemicial fertilizers are the most essential input for modern agriculture. Fertilizer consumption has increased considerably. From almost zero level per hectare consumption in 1950-51, the consumption in 1986-87 was estimated to have gone up to 48.44 kg per hectare. India ranks as world's fourth largest producer of nitrogen fertilizer and the fifth largest producer of phosphatic fertilizer. At present the consumption of NPK in the country is 10.3 million tonnes. By the year 2000 the demand for fertilizers will go up to 20 million tonnes to help produce the projected food grain requirements of 240 million tonnes in order to feed the growing population.

Such large input of chemical fertilizes will create diverse problems of environmental pollution which can be grouped into two categories.

1. Pollution caused during fertilizer production; and
2. Pollution resulting from the use of fertilizers

In the manufacture of fertilizers, large amounts of gaseous and liquid effluents are generated as by-products. The pollution cause by such effluents is relatively localized and can be remedied by reducing the volume of effluents or by treating them before their release into the environment. The Central and State Pollution Control Boards are persuading fertilizer manufacturers to cut down the release of effluents by enforcing Minimum National Effluent Standards prescribed for the fertilizer industry.

The application of fertilizers in the field created many complex problems of environmental pollution. A substantial portion of the fertilizers applied to the field is los through runoff, leaching, gasification or biological transformation. Runoff from agricultural fields laden with plant nutrients and excessive fertilizer water bodies is a condition technically called eutrophication. Over-loading water bodies with plant nutrients over-stimulates and disturbs the ecological Leakage of the ecosystems. Leakage of nitrate into the ground water creates the danger of nitrate poisoning. The problem of environmental pollution caused by the allocation of fertilizers in the field are widespread and difficult to control. Pollution loads build up in the environment in a field are widespread wand difficult to control. pollution loads build up in the environment in a cumulative manner, bypassing the existing pollution control legislations. The anticipated intensification of agriculture in the future is going to magnify the problems of environmental pollution in the coming decades.

Pesticides

Pesticides are a group of chemicals used for controlling pests, insects, weeds, disease-causing bacteria, fungi and viruses. The organochlorine compounds, which include insecticides like adlrin, dieldrin. DDT and its derivatives, are causing great concern to environmentalists. DDT is highly resistant and gets widely dispersed throughout the ecosystem. It is present in rainfall, soil and in wildlife dispersed throughout deer and the Arctic penguin. It is soluble in fat and hence, tends to accumulate in very large quantities in the liver of animals occupying the higher levels in the food chain, e.g., man, birds of prey,etc.

The use of pesticides in India has grown rapidly since independence DDT and BHC are the two main pesticides used in large quantities, DDT has been very effective against insect pests that destroy crops and insect vectors transmit malaria and plague. Since the cropped area under plant protection has increased from 6.4 million hectares in 1960-61 to over 80 million hatchets in 1980, the average consumption of pesticides increased from 3.2 g/ha in 1954-55 to 336 g/ha in 1980. The use of these agrochemicals is going to increase in future. The success of pesticides has been a mixed blessing because their use has serious environmental implications. In 1962 Rahcal Carson, in her famous book, *Silent Spring*, highlighted the dangers of introducing large quantities of non-specific pesticides.

A comparative evaluation of DDT in human fat tissue from different countries shockingly revealed that residents in Delhi had very high levels of DDT, DDT and BHC have been found to be abundantly present in samples of butter and wheat flour collected from Punjab. Even mother's milk has been found to be contaminated with DDT. Both DDT and BHC have a lot of residue toxicity and can even cause cancer.

Pesticide use therefore should be strictly controlled and regulated. With a view to controlling the sale and use of pesticides, the government of India passed an Insecticide Act in 1968, but it has been poorly implemented.

Unimaginative mining

Mining is an extractive process. Coal, lignite, iron-ire, limestone and bauxite are mainly obtained for surface mining. The Indian mining industry is expanding at a steady rate of around 5 percent. The value of mineral production increased from Rs. 85 crore in 1951 to Rs, 9953 crore in the year 1987.

Mining operations induce serious hydrological disturbances, as some of the aquifers may be intercepted by mine openings. The underground hydrological system is greatly disturbed. Dewatering of mine pits causes water pollution of streams and reservoirs. The Damodar river in Bhowrah has turned black in colour due to suspended solid discharged by the coal washeries in Jharia. Water of many streams in the Bihar-Orrisa iron-ore belt is redish yellow due to the discharge of iron-ore fine and lateritic slimes. Also water pollution sometimes occurs due to breaches or overflowing of tailing ponds. The influx of labour engaged in mining creates problems of water pollution due to the discharge of raw sewage.

Dust generated by mining and blasting operations, by the movement of heavy earth-moving equipment and by over- burdened dumps, contributes to air pollution. Diesel operated equipments, such as shovel, dumper, tractor,etc. release lots of Co, SO_2, No_x and aldehydes into the environment.

Mining and mineral processing have a great impact on the environment. Open-cast mining is highly devastating and leads to large scale environmental degradation. Limestone mining in th Mussoorie-Dehradum region and bauxite mining by the Bharat Alumnimum Company in the Gandhmardan hills in Orrisa, have led to widespread public outcry against the environmental degradation. The main environmental problems caused by open-cast or surface mining are: deforestation, wildlife destruction, land damage, hydrological disturbances, water and air pollution, noise and ground vibrations, displacement of population, socio-economic changes and aesthetic blight. Although the actual mining is carried out in a relatively small area, its impact spills over to a much larger area.

In open-cast mining the mineral is obtained by removing the overlying non-ore material. Huge piles of over-burden keep growing around the mine pit creating a 'hill and dale' topography. Over-burden and digout pits are abandoned after the mining excavation is over, since there is no legal obligation foe reclaiming the area after mining is over. Mining brings in additional traffic load in the area, leading to the road congestion as well as increase in noise levels. Moreover, eviction of local inhabitants from the ore-bearing area leads to serious socio-economic distortions. The phenomenon of environmental refugees as a result of such environmental degradation poses serious problems. The ancillary and down-stream industries, drawn by the mining activities, case further deterioration of the environment.

Water pollution

Water is the life-blood of the environment. Without water no living thing, plant, animal or man can survive. The availability of an adequate and usable supply of water underpins our whole economy. Water is used for transportation and power generation, for waste disposal, recreation, agriculture, and fisheries. It is essential both for the manufacturing and the service sectors.

Requirements of fresh water for different uses during 1974 and the estimated figures for the years 2000 and 2025 are give in the following Table.

Table Water use of major activities in India, 1974-2025.

Use	1974	2000	2025
Irrigation	350	630	770
Domestic & Livestock	13	34	50
Industries	5	30	120
Thermal power generation	10	60	160

It may be seen that by the beginning of the twenty first century, there will be a six times increase in the water required for industry, and by the year 2025 it will be 24 times the present demand. A rational pragmatic strategy for the management and recycling of water needed to cope with such galloping demands. The problem of great concern. Water pollution is the most important cause of public health problems, both in rural and urban areas. The frequent eruption of epidemics are caused by the pollution of drinking water. Waterborne diseases, such as cholera, typhoid, diarrhoea, dysentery, malaria, and intestinal worms claim a heavy toll every year. Inadequate hygiene, poor sanitation and discharge of industrial effluents have resulted in the pollution of many of our surface water sources.

The main sources of water pollution are summarized as: (1) urban/domestic effluents; (2) industrial liquid effluents; (3) surface runoff from cultivated fields where fertilizers, pesticides, insecticides and other agro-chemicals are used; (4) surface runoff from urban and industrial solid-waste dumping areas; and (5) nuclear and thermal plant discharges.

Domestic wastes constitute approximately 90 per cent of total pollution load, while 7 per cent from large and medium industries and 3 per cent from small scale industries. In Delhi, domestic wastes constitute approximately 98 per cent by volume. In Bombay, the industrial capital of india, it is approximately 84 pcr cent.

The Sabarmati is the most polluted river of the country with a BOD (Biological Oxygen Demant) level of 1655 mg/1. The Mahi, the Narmada, the Tapti, the Krishna, the Cauvery, the Pennar, the Godavari and the Subarnarekha rivers are also polluted in stretches. All the major rivers immediately downstream of big cities are polluted. The Ganga river is most seriously polluted near Kanpur, Varanasi and Howrah. The BOD levels in Varanasi and Kanpur are at times reported to be higher than 30 mg/1.

The status of sewage control and treatment in Class I cities and in Class II cities is very precarious. India's progress in controlling domestic wastes, as surveyed during 1978-80 is indicated.

As regards water pollution caused by industries. 17 categories of industries have been identified as contributing to it. Out of the 1.700 large and medium scale industries identified as water polluters, approximately 800 have established pollution abatement devices.

Table Status of disposal of domestic waste water

Class of City or Town	*Number*	*Sewered*	*Unsewered (Percent)*	*Waste water volume (millions of liters/day) Generated*	*collected*	*Treated*
Class I	142	43	57	7.000	598	378
Class II	198	12	88	1,200	158	58

Ocean pollution

Ocean and coastal areas have also suffered from the pressure of growing human population. They are being used as convenient dumping sites of all kinds of water, including toxic and hazardous materials, without giving much thought to the consequences. In addition, the use of sea routes for transporting oil cargo causes problem of oil pollution of the marine environment. One of the important oil tanker routes passes through the Arabian Sea and Southern Bay of Bengal and it lies close to our western sea coast. Leakages and oil spills from tankers are the prime causes of oil pollution of the marine environment. Resides, when tankers are involved in accidents, the impact on ocean water is still more serious. Crude oil, being immiscible and lighter than water, quickly spreads and floats over the sea surface. Oil slicks are carried to the shore by sea currents. An oil cover on the sea surface blocks the free exchange of gases between sea water and the atmosphere. Floating oil slicks chocke the gills of fish and clog the plumage of marine birds. In short, the communities of marine organisms are completely destroyed. Offshore drilling and oil production yet another potential threat for scale oil pollution of the marine environment.

Recent satellite surveys suggest that the oil pollution of the Arabian Sea has increased considerably. Beaches along the west coast of India are plagued with tar-ball deposition which adversely affects their use as recreation spots and discourages tourism. Clean-up operations are very expensive, cumbersome, inefficient and are rarely carried out. Consequently, oil pollution of the marine environment generates several complex problems.

Air pollution

Air pollution is one of the major problems. It is caused by moving and point sources. Moving sources are represented by automobiles, ships, aircrafts and rockets. Industries and thermal power plants are examples of point sources of air pollution.

The burning of fossil fuel products oxides of sulphur, nitrogen carbon dioxide, carbon monoxide and a complex mixture of organic compounds along with particulate matter. The most important pollutants in the Indian environment are suspended particulate matter and So_2. The SPM levels in most of the urban areas are beyond the permissible level. In fact, an unpleasant pall of dust has become almost an integral part of urban areas. Air pollution problems are most visible. They affect living organisms significantly. Apart from creating problems of poor visibility, dust pollution causes respiratory diseases particularly in children and elderly persons.

Sulphur dioxide is the most important among

the gaseous pollutants. It is released by thermal power plants and other industries along with a large amount of flyash. The problem of flyash and SPM pollution caused by power plants, cement and other industries, can be controlled by their installing electrostatic precipitators. The gaseous pollutants, however, escape into the atmosphere. Growing consumption of fossil fuels has enormous implications for the air quality. An estimate made some time ago indicates that SO_2 emission from fossil fuels ins the country has increased from 1.4 tonnes in 1964 to 3.2 m tonnes in 1979. It is expected to increase further as the tempo of industrial development gains momentum. Sulphur dioxide affects all living organisms, but plant are particularly vulnerable to this gas.

The average content of lead in the environment is increasing. Tera-ethy lead is added in petrol as an anti-knock agent. A study carried out in Delhi has revealed that the lead content in the ambient air near the road side varied between 90 to 324 narogarms per cubic meter, while its value never exceeded 62ng/m in the background station located away from vehicular traffic.

Acid rain

Acid ráin, which has emerged as the great scourge in the industrial countries, is regarded an imminent threat to India, where the emission of acidic gases is sharply increasing. In the last few decades the rain water has become acidic over large areas in Europe and North America. The term 'Acid Rain' is used to describe all precipitation rain, snow, sleet, dew which are more acidic than normal. Acid deposition is caused when sulphur and nitrogen oxides from coal and oil fired power plants, from industrial processes, such as metal smelting, and from motor vehicle exhausts, combine in the atmosphere with water vapour, sunlight and oxygen to form sulphuric and nitric acids. Environmèntal acidification, is thus, a man-made phenomenon. Emission of sulphur dioxide and oxide of nitrogen are prime contributors to atmospheric acidification, as they readily dissolve in the atmospheric moisture forming sulphuric and nitric acids which make the rain acidic.

The ecological impacts of acid precipitation are far-reaching, insidious and often produce irreversible changes. Acid rain has a corroding effect on plant leaves and thus pre-disposes them to pests, pathogens and other environmental stresses. The soil becomes acidic-a condition which releases toxic heavy metal ions in the soil and promotes the loss of calcium and magnesium from the soil. the cumulative effect is the gradual degradation of soil and a decline in forest productivity. In aquatic systems, acidic rain raises the levels of toxic heavy metals resulting in the death of fish and the reproductive failure. Increased acidity of lakes and streams prevents hatching of fish eggs and kills they young fry. Acidification in industrialized countries is responsible for making thousands of lakes unproductive, turning them into virtual biological deserts.

The vast expansion of thermal power generation and other industrial activities contribute to environmental acidification. The release of sulphur dioxide and oxides of nitrogen are rapidly increasing in the Indian environment and this trend is going to intensify in the future due to growing demands of our galloping population. Systematic and reliable data on the acidity of rain water In india are lacking, but occasionally acid rain has been reported from Bombay, Delhi, Nagpur, Pune and a few other station.

Green house effect

Carbon dioxide is a natural constituent of the atmosphere and has concentration of a little over 0.032 per cent by volume, a ratio of 1 to 450 with oxygen. in spite of its relatively small proportion, carbon dioxide plays a very important and useful role in the biosphere until its ratio is disturbed. It is like glass, transparent to visible light but absorbing the infra-red radiations. It lets the sun's rays through to the earth, but traps the heat that would otherwise be radiated back into space. While the natural levels of carbon dioxide keep the earth's temperature at a comfortable 15 C. any increase in its level makes the earth hotter.

It is in view of this phenomenon that a great concern is growing because of the steadily increasing carbon dioxide concentration in the atmosphere. It is estimated that from 1700 to 1975 the concentration of carbon dioxide in the atmosphere has increased from 270 ppm to 334 ppm. Its over-all concentration has increased by nearly twenty five per cent since the process of industrialisation started in the world. Most scientists are therefore in agreement that global warming is underway. This phenomenon is known as the 'Green House Effect". Besides carbon dioxide, other trace gases like methane, nitrous oxide, the chloro-fluoro-carbons and ozone also produce the Green house Effect and have an additive action. What will be the environmental impact of this phenomenon? How will plants, animals or ecosystems as a whole respond to it?

Precise predictions are difficult, but significant studies indicate that die to a global increase in carbon dioxide, the temperature of the lower atmosphere is likely to increase by 1.5 C to 45 C by the year 2030. This would lead to a rise in the global sea level because of two major reasons. First, the rise in atmospheric temperature will make the average temperature of the oceans warmer. Because of this heat transfer, the water of the earth will expand. Second, the rising temperature will result in the melting of polar ice caps, which will ultimately result in the rise of the sea level. Empirical studies predict that global warming would lead to a rise in sea level between 1.4 metres to 2.2 meters by the end of this century. This would have obvious implications to millions of people living in coastal areas and delta regions of rivers like the Ganges.

Increasing carbon dioxide will induce sweeping changes in the biosphere. Plants will be affected by the rising levels of 'green house gases' in two ways. First, the high concentration of carbon dioxide will have a fertilising effect and will encourage plant growth. Second, the concomitant increase in the ambient temperature will include long0-term climate change. Climate shift will upset the present day cropping pattern over large northward. Insects will breed faster. Many wetlands will dry out, some food chains will be altered and broken or some will disappear. the over-all impact will be distressing.

Ozone depletion

Ozone is a deep blue gas made up of chemically bonded oxygen atoms and is a minor constituent of the earth's atmosphere. It is found everywhere between sea level and a height of 60km in varying concentrations. In the air we breathe, ozone is a health hazard, a constituent of air pollution that has a caustic effect on human skin. However, in the stratosphere, ozone forms and delicate veil, filtering out UV radiation from sun's rays entering the earth's atmosphere. In fact the presence of an ozone layer in the stratosphere is vital for life on earth because it is the only natural shield against UV radiation, which is a potent mutagenic agent.

It has recently, been discovered that the protective ozone layer is getting progressively eroded due to the impact of increasing human interference with the environment. A significant reduction in ozone layer over Antarctica is already a matter of concern. The major cause for the depletion of the ozone layer is the worldwide emission of man-made compounds called cholorofluoro-carbon. Chloro-fluoro-carbons are used in refrigerators, air conditioners, acrosols, sprays, for the cleaning of computer chips, and in the making of rubber foam and polystyrene containers required for food packaging. CFCs are by and large chemically inert, having no direct effect on humans or other lying organisms. After their release they ultimately find their way to the stratosphere where they chemically react with ozone molecules, breaking them down. If the release of CFCs continues at the current rate, the ozone layer will be further depleted and living organisms, including human beings, will be exposed to higher levels of UV radiation. Scientists believe that increased doses of UV radiation will cause eyes damage, skin cancer, and will accelerate the aging process both in humans and domestic stock at all latitudes. The seriousness of ozone depletion is similar to the hazards of nuclear disaster. It is urgently necessary to prevent further damage to the ozone layer.

Efforts to improve quality of environment

In India there has been a growing realisation of the impact of the increasing population and accelerated development strategies on the quality of the environment. The increasing human demands have been exerting great pressure on the natural resource base, agricultural land, energy sources, vital watersheds, forests, etc... resulting in environmental degradation. Recurring natural calamities, such as floods and droughts, have attracted the attention of one and all. The concern was well reflected in the Parliament when a specific provision on protection and improvement of the environment and safeguarding of forests and wildlife was added to the chapter on directive Principles of State Policy by the Constitution Act, 1976.

Article 48 A of this chapter states: 'The State shall endeavour to protect and improve the environment and to safeguard the forests and wildlife of the country.'

This constitutional amendment further evidenced the concern of the Members of Parliament for environmental improvement by incorporating Part IV A on Fundamental Duties which provides for a duty of citizens to the environment. In its Article 51 A Constitution states: 'It shall be the duty of every citizen of india ...(g) to protect and improve the natural environment including forests, lakes, rivers and wildlife, and to have compassion for living creatures.

However, the official concern for the environment was expressed for the first time in the Fourth five Year Plan Document, which emphasised the need to introduce environmental dimension into the development planning process. In 1972 a Committee on environmental Planning and Coordination was set up to advise the government on all environmental matters. In January 1980 another Committee was set up to suggest legislative measures and an administrative machinery for ensuring environmental protection. On the recommendations of this Committee, the Department of Environment was set up by the Government. Subsequently, a separate Ministry of Environment and Forests was established in 1985 to deal with various environmental matters. the government has initiated a number of measures to protect and upgrade the environment.

Thirty major enactments related to the protection of the environment are now being administered by the central and state governments. The Water Act, 1974 and the Air Act 1981, the Factories Act, and the Insecticide Act are some of the prominent ones among these enactments. The Bhopal gas tragedy in 1984 came as a rude shock and it exposed the dangers of hazardous chemicals. A Union Carbide pesticide plant accidentally released a cloud of deadly methy I isocyanate over the town. This accident killed about 2500 and more than 200,00 people fled for their lives. Nearly 100,000 people are still suffering from various kinds of side effects, such an blurred vision, lung diseases, intestinal bleeding and neurological disorders. This led the Government to enact the Environment Protection Act to deal with the environmental matters in a comprehensive manner and to plug the loopholes in the existing legislations.

The governments has made it mandatory that environmental issues and unintended ecological side effects of the proposed development projects are identified in advance and necessary corrective measures are incorporate to reduce the undesirable environmental impact. Project approval by the Ministry of Environment and Forests often requires implementation of suggested safeguards and mitigative measures. The Central and State pollution control Boards have been constituted. The Central Board has prescribed minimum national standards for liquid and gaseous effluents in respect of 12 major polluting industries. An ongoing programme of monitoring and assessment of air and water quality is being carried out to keep a close watch on the emerging trends. There are a number of critical environmental challenges that are being met by undertaking suitable measures.

Countering deforestation

Soon after independence in 1974, the Government of India took note of the extensive destruction of the forest wealth of the country. In order to reverse this trend and to arouse public consciousness about the importance of forest in the welfare of the nation, an annual tree planting festival was started in 1950. Since then each year, tree planting campaigns have been undertaken while celebrating 'Van Mohotsava'. In the early years there was a great enthusiasm and the response of the people was quite encouraging. Unfortunately, over the years it has lost its vigour reducing it to a mere ritual without much impact. The concept of 'Van Mahotsava' is highly relevant but unfortunately it has entered into deep dormancy.

Deforestation has been occurring for many

years and about half of the area under forests sin the country is degraded. Ecological restoration of damanged areas is needed for meeting the socio-economic needs of the people. The National Agriculture commission recommended that 'Social Forestry' be undertaken to meet the fuel-wood, fodder and small timber needs to rural communities. The main objectives of social forestry are to relieve the pressure on existing forests,s to promote the productive use of public and common lands in a decentralized manner, to promote soil and water conservation and to create employment opportunities in rural areas. It envisages creation of local village level nurseries and involvement of the local population including women and children to raise trees of their choice to meet their needs. This includes the planting of trees on denuded and even on agricultural lands inter-mixed with crop plants or along farm boundaries or on vacant lands, Depending on local conditions, it can take any one of the following emphases: Agri-silvicltural, Agri-pastoral or Agri-silvipastoral.

The government has been laying considerable empphasis on social forestry programmes since 1986 and fund allocation for this purpose has been steadily growing. Tree seedlings are being distributed free to the poor people in rural states to give usufruct rights over trees planted and protected on public lands by the rural poor. The usufruct rights provide the individuals the right to use the trees and get profit out of them, but they cannot be regarded as their property. Until recently, tree planting and afforestation programmes have remained mostly confined to quick-growing trees like Eucalyptus or the commercial species. This has increased the raw material supply instead of mitigating shortages of fuel-wood and fodder.

To bring about qualitative changes in the programme, in June, 1988, the national waste-lands Development Board was set up with the principal aim of regenerating wasteland through massive afforestation and tree planting. Waste-land maps have been prepared for 146 selected districts in 19 states, showing village-wise distribution of 13 categories of Wastelands. Village-specific action plans identifying land treatments, if any, need to be prepared. The future programme would focus on drylands for the production of fuel-wood, fodder and small timber on public lands an multiple purpose trees under farm forestry.

The Government of india announced a comprehensive National Forest Policy in December 1988. The principal aim of the new policy is to ensure environmental stability and equilibrium, which are vital for sustenance of all life forms, human, animal and plant. The derivation of direct economic benefits must be subordinated to this principal aim. A great deal of organisation effort will be needed for the successful implementation of this policy.

People's participation

Enlightened public opinion and active involvement of people is necessary for protecting and improving the local environment. A local leader, Chandiprashad Bhatt started a practical and non-violent methods- the 'Chipko Movement'- to save the forest of Uttarakhand from the axes of contractors. On 27 March, 1973 the residents of Mandal village of Chamóli district lid not allow as sports goods manufacturing firm of Allahabad to fell the sash trees auctioned to them by the U.P. government. The sports company moved towards Mandakini Valley of the Kedarnath region. But there too they met with similar resistance. Hill women and children showed remarkable courage and joined the 'Chipko Movement' and successfully save the village trees from felling.

The 'Chipko Movement' highlighted the value of conservation over the extraction of temporary economic benefits trees. a new slogan was given, namely 'What do the forests bear?. Soil, water and pure air. Soil, water and pure air are the basis of life. ' A massive planting of trees was started to provide the Five 'Fs'-food, fodder, fuel, fertilizer and fiber. Within a few years, the 'Chipko Movement' developed into a powerful mass- based ecological movement in the country.

Protecti on of wild plants and animals

Various animal species and plants are great assets for the future well-being of society. Wild plants and animals have provided breeding materials for improving the commercially useful species. A few instances will display their invaluable contribution to human welfare and prosperity. A wild melon from India provided the genes for resistance to mildew of a melon crop as far away as in California in the united States. A wild rice collected in 1963 in Uttar Pradesh gave the genes which saved 30 million hectares of paddy from grassy sweet virus. The *'Kaus'* grass from Indonesia provided the genes for resistance to redrot disease of sugarcane. Among animals, the showl cows of Punjab and Haryana and the goat of Etah district of Uttar Pradesh have been utilised for improving the breeds of these animals in many countries.

Penicillium, a microscopic of soil fungus, which is a source of the popular antibiotic Penicillin and *Cinchona*, from which quinine is obtained , were unnoticed species until their useful properties were discovered. What a great loss it would have been if these two species had become extinct before the discovery of their medicinal value. Our knowledge about the majority of wild plants and animals is very limited, and hence loosing them without knowing their virtue will be a great tragedy.

But deforesation, poaching, monoculture, pollution and habitat destruction have already caused extinction of many species of plants and animals. The widespread use of selected high-yielding varieties of crop plants as well as mechanisation of agriculture had dangerously eroded the genetic diversity of agriculturally viable species. According to an estimate, the number of endangered species of flowering plants in the country has sharply risen from hundreds to thousands over the past few years. It is no feared that 10 to 20 per cent i.e. over 2500 species of the total vascular plants, may now fall in one or the other categories to threatened species. All species, whether they are economically useful or not and whether their economic uses are known or not, are crucial importance in the ecosystem.

Long term measures directed towards conservation are necessary for protecting the plants and animals. The conservation of threatened and endangered wildlife species is best achieved when their natural habitats are protected. In our country a number of natural areas have been set aside with a view to conserve various endangered wildlife species. There are now sixty-seven National Parks and 394 Sanctuaries distributed all over the country, representing 4 per cent of the total geographical area. They cover a wide range of ecosystems ranging from forests, grasslands, deserts, river basins, lakes, wetlands, mangroves and marine areas. Special efforts have been made to conserve the magnificent tiger, which is our national animal, by establishing 17 tiger reserves, covering an area of 26,634 sq. km. in 13 states.

It is now increasingly recognised that conservation of wild areas along with the inherent diversity of their plants, animals, insects and micro-organisms is vital for sustainable development. Long-term conservation of the representative ecosystems of the country has been initiated by creating four Biosphere Reserves namely, the Nilgiris, Nanda Devi, Nokrok and

Great Nicobar. Another nine potential biosphere sites have been identified.

Recycling of resources

Almost all facets of human activity produce large quantities of undesirable by products which are called wastes. For every ton of grain, fruit or vegetable produced, between tow and three tonnes of solid waste are generated .

Based on a 'global average', it has been calculated that a city of one million inhabitants generates 500,000 metric tonnes of waste water, 2,00 metric tonnes of solid wastes and 950 metric tonnes of air pollutants every day. The quality and variety of wastes are growing with urban and industrial expansion. Waste disposal is becoming a major concern demanding a substantial share from the budgets of civic bodies. Waste disposal, being non-remunerative, is usually treated with neglect, resulting in the piling up of waste heaps in towns and cities resulting in frequent outbreaks of epidemics.

This need not be so, if waste recycling is practiced and by-product utilization is taken up seriously. Nature does it for itself all the time. In sharp contrast to human societies, recyling is a norm in nature, hence the problem of waste is non-existent. For example, green plants utilize carbon dioxide produced by other living organisms or released from the decomposition of dead plants and animals.

Wastes are of two types, namely organic and

inorganic. They can be potential sources of materials or energy or both, provided they are imaginatively recycled. Wastes recycling and utilization can take any one or more of th following forms, namely retrieval of useful material, resource separation, energy recovery and innovative utilization.

Waste picking is an established practice in urban and industrial areas. Useful, materials such as glass bottles, containers and metal scrap are recovered and sold. A 10 MW capacity thermal power plant is already operating using rice husk in Punjab. Similarly bagasse is another potential source of energy. A 3.75 MW plant has been installed din Delhi to generate power from the incineration of the city waste.

It has been convincingly demonstrated that cattle dung, human excreta, agricultural and domestic wastes are suitable feed-stock for biogas generation. In the Okhla area of New Delhi the city sewage is utilized for generating biogas which is supplied to the nearby colonies ad domestic fuel.

Innovative waste utilization

Large quantities of flyash produced in coal-fired thermal power plants can be used for variety of purposes such as for the production of cement and bricks, for applying as soleing-material for roads and air strips and for using as building material. Waste recycling and reuse are essential for resource conservation, environmental. Waste recycling and reuse are essential for resource conservation, environmental improvement and sustainable development. The following examples indicate the patterns of the implications involved in the recycling process.

Composting: Considerable amount of agricultural and animal wastes are traditionally composted and used as farm yard manure in villages. But with the advent of inorganic fertilizers, this practice if fading way over the years.

Land Fills: In almost all towns and cities, the most common method of disposing solid waste is by using it for land filling and land reclamation. In big cities like Calcutta, Bombay, Delhi and Madras several residential flats have been constructed by reclaiming land through this process. This is seldom carried out scientifically and hence the land fill sites become potentially dangerous to public health.

Cleaning up the Ganges

The Ganges, one of the most celebrated and revered rivers in the world, is also one of the most polluted. Almost one-third of the country's population lives in the Ganga basin. Out of 100 towns and cities situated along its banks, 20 per cent represent major urban conglomerations. The rapid growth of these centres has led to over-exploitation of the rivers, leading to rapid degradation of the river water quality.

Some 600 km of its total length are dangerously polluted with human, animal, agricultural and industrial wastes. The majority of villages, towns and cities suited on the banks of the Ganga have no sewage treatment plants and, even if they exist, they are far too small, badly maintained and poorly operated. Frequently water flows through open drains into the Ganga. Experts say that if sewage discharge alone could be stopped, pollution levels of the river would drop by 75 percent. Contamination of water by sewage is the principal cause of water-borne diseases, including cholera, typhoid and para-typhoid fever, dysentery and infectious hepatitis. In addition to sewage, dead bodies, half cremated corpses, dead animals and synthetic detergents are additional factors responsible for destroying the health of the river Ganga. detergents release large amounts of phosphates, which over-fertilize the river water, leading to many undesirable effects on the water quality.

The practice of intensive agriculture in the Ganga basin has greatly promoted the consumption of chemical fertilizers. The Ganga is constantly fed by surface run-off from cultivated lands which have been treated with excessive amounts of fertilizer and manure. A two-year study conducted by the Central Pollution Control Board indicates that 1.15 m tonnes of pesticides were applied in the Ganga Basin- an amount equal to 34 per cent of India's annual consumption. A large proportion of this ultimately finds its way to the Ganga through run-off waters.

Recognizing the need to protect human health and the ecology of the river, the government of India has launched a major clean-up programme, called the Ganga Action Plan. Over the next five years, the government has commuted Rs. 250 crores for the rehabilitation of the river.

During the first phase of the action plan, a number of measures have been undertaken. A number of projects are being implemented to renovate the existing sewage systems in all towns and cities along the Ganga to upgrade all existing sewage treatment and pumping plants, to install new sewage treatment plants wherever necessary and to extend sewage line into areas not currently covered by the treatment network. These projects also relate to the construction of large community cattle sheds in urban areas to collect animal wastes for biogas and fertilizer and regulation of the use and application of pesticides and chemical fertilizers in agriculture in the watershed of the Ganga to minimise surface run-off.

One of the important features of the Ganga Action Plan, therefore, is to recover and recycle the organic wastes for useful proposes. Sewage is a very rich source of energy and of organic manure. A proper sewage treatment plant can yield both energy as biogas and slurry which can be used as an organic manure.

Natural resources: Rational utilisation

The interrelationships between population, resources and environment are very complex. It demands a consummate understanding for appreciating the linkages that are crucial for sustainable development. However, it is universally accepted that human survival depends on resources like air, soil, water, forest wildlife and minerals, which nature has bestowed on us. It is also being increasingly realised that rapid population growth has resulted in great pressure on natural resources.

Let us examine the potentials and limitations of our natural resources, which can be grouped into *living* and *non-living* resources. They can also be categroised on the basis of their inherent characteristics into two categories, namely *renewable* and *non-renewable* resources. Some resources are inexhaustible and keep on renewing themselves if managed properly. These are known as renewable resources. But resources like coal, petroleum, etc. are non-renewable, as the stock of these resources is fixed and with constant use their quantities decrease. The regeneration capacity of even renewable resources is seriously impaired, or many even be lost, if these are not properly managed. Extinction of plant and animal species, desertification, soil erosion and salinisation are examples of renewable resources becoming non-renewable through overuse and excessive exploitation.

The natural reserves of metals and minerals are fixed and finite. Strictly speaking they are non- destructible and can be recycled repeatedly. But in practice they get dissipated and dispersed through human use. Sometimes metals are used any once metal is cumbersome or expensive. It is therefore very much desirable that natural resources are conserved and managed wisely to avoid their wastage or under utilization. The conservation and efficient utilization of living and non-living resources is vital for meeting the demands of the growing population. The status of some important natural resources is deiscussed in the following section.

Mineral resources

Mineral resources greatly contribute to the generation of wealth. Our country is richly endowed with minerals. India is self-sufficient in 35 minerals which are used as raw materials by various industries. Table 6.3 gives an idea of the available quantities of some important minerals in the country. The main mineral producing states are Bihar, Madhya Pradesh, West Bengal, Gujarat, Rajashthan and Adndra Pradesh.

The mining and mineral industry has steadily grown during the past years. The mineral production in 1976 was worth Rs. 1,365 crore and it rose to Rs. 9,641 crore in 1986. The share of fuel minerals, non-metallic minerals and metallic minerals was worth Rs. 8,226, Rs. 770 and Rs. 644 crore respectively. The major mining operations in india are open-cast, which severely affect the land-use pattern in the area. Land subsidence in underground mining areas affects the general landscape very adversely.

Coal

The total coal resources in India according to the estimate made by the geological Survey of India is 117 billion tonnes. Out of this, 86,427 million tonnes can be categorised under reserves. These consist of coal seams situated upto 600 metres of depth and more than 1.2 meters in thickness. About 5.094 million tonnes of coal deposits can be categorised under conditional resources which cannot be mined under present-day technological options. The balance resources are distributed between speculative and hypothetical resources depending upon the degree of certainty in the exploration of deposits.

Table Estimated reserves of some important mineral resources in India

Mineral	*Estimated Reserves in Crore tonnes*
Bauxite	265.37
Chromite	13.53
Copper Ore	57.60
Diamond	10.00
Dolomite	395.00
Gold	148.51
Fire Clay	49.28
Gypsum	124.86
Graphite	46.41
Iron Ore	19.757
Lead Sin	35.85
Limestone	7.320
Manganese	13.50
Nickel Ore	23.13
Tungstan	71.00
Refrctory Minerals:	
(Magnesite, Kyanite, sillimanite)	23.91

Estimated Reserves in lakh tonnes

The proven coal reserves in the country are of the order of 156 billion tonnes. The actual coal production in the country has increased from

55.67 million tonnes in 1960-61 to 180 million tonnes in 1988-89. By 2004-04 the coal production is expected to increase up to 450 million tonnes per annum. Almost two-thirds of this will be from open-cast mines and one-third will be from underground mines.

Petroleum

The balance recoverable reserves of oil and natural gas in the country are at present estimated at 58.1 crore tonnes and 541 billion cubic metres respectively. The annual production of crude oil was around 320 lakh tonnes in 1987 and that of natural gas was bout 981.2 crore cubic meters in 1986-87. The balance recoverably reserves of natural gas increased from 35,200 crore cubic meters as on January, 1980 to 54,100 crore cubic meter in January 1987. The present requirement of petroleum products is in excess of domestic availability and the shortfall of about 6 to 17 million tonnes is being met through imports. The demand for petroleum products is expected to rise to about 111 million tonnes by the year 2004-05, whereas the domestic production is likely to attain a level of only about 58 million tonnes. We will, therefore, have to continue to depend on imports to meet a substantIal part of our demand for petroleum products in the coming years. The position in respect of the availability of natural gas is, however, expected to improve considerably over the coming years and the reserves of natural gas in the country are expected to last much longer than those of crude oil. In 1987 there were 12 refineries in the country having a total capacity of 467.00 lakh tonnes.

Energy

Power is the most basic requirement for industrial and economic development. The total energy consumption of 186.3 million tonnes of coal replacement in 1953-54 has grown to about 750 million tonnes of coal requirement in 1988 and is expected to rise to 1224 million tonnes by the year 2000.

The power generation scenario shows that thermal power is most important modality followed by hydro-electric power, while nuclear power contributes only about per cent to the total power output. In the foreseeable future, the contribution of thermal power is going to grow further while the relative position of hydro-electric and nuclear power generation will remain the same. The environmental impacts of these different types of power generation are discussed below.

Environmental impact of thermal power generation: Thermal power generation has a wide variety of direct and indirect effects on the environment. The direct effects are due to the combustion of coal which gives rise to a number of air-borne effluents, the most important of which are sulphur oxide, nitrogen oxide, carbon monoxide, carbon dioxide, particulates, organic compounds, trace metal and radionuclides.

Substantial amounts of nitrogen oxides, are generally present in the effluent gases. The source of nitrogen oxides is not the fuel *per se* but the nitrogen in the air combines with the oxygen in the air during the combustion process to produce NO. Later, most of the NO oxides to NO_2, which in turn, can combine with water to form nitric acid aernsol.

Environmental aspects of hydro-electric generation Hydro-electric generation has a number of environmental impacts. No dam can be built and no impoundment can be created without affecting the environment. A dam becomes a dominant factor in the hydrological regime, and sets in motion a series of impacts on physical, biological and socio-cultural systems. The dam and the lake behind it cause many effects on the environment regardless of the dam's geographical location. The environmental side-effects of dam construction are generally divided into two categories: (a) the local effects and the reactions within the area of the man-made lake, and (b) the downstream effect resulting from a change in the hydraulic regime. Both types of side-effects of hydro-electric generation have a complex impact on the physical, bilogical and socio-economic environment:

The folding of the region could have immediate and significant impact on the means of communication, historic sites, communities which are inundated, and the local flora and fauna. In this connection the Silent valley represents and excellent example. A hydro-electric dam was proposed to be constructed in the Palghat district of kerala. The project involved the construction of an RCC arch dam of a georage formed by two hillocks rising approximately 160 to 250 meters above the bed level. The dam was supposed to submerge over 670 hectares of virgin tropical rain forest, which to the project proponents was not very important. Ecologically, the area represents the highest expression of mother nature and there are hardly and obstacle, not only to the free running of water, but also to fish migration and evolutionary work of nature, and in view of the overwhelming ecological considerations, the silent valley project was dropped altogether.

Environmental impact of nuclear power generation: Environmental hazards of nuclear power have been the subject of heated debate the world over. The environmental consequences of nuclear power generation are most complex and potentially dangerous.

The health hazards of radiation are the consequences of alpha and beta particles and gamma rays emitted by radioactive materials. These particles and rays can permanently change the hereditary materials of cells in living organisms, thereby inducing cancer. Firm evidence suggests that people who have been exposed to low level radiation over extended periods of time show an increased incidence of leukemia, skin, thyroid and lung cancer. For example, studies of children who have received X-ray treatments in the neck region have shown an increased incidence of thyroid cancer. Generally, a five-to-twenty-year latency period elapses following exposure before these diseases are diagnosed.

Low level exposure also accelerates the ageing

process, thus shortening life span, and can cause chromosimic damage. The human foetus is particularly susceptible to radiation damage.

Exposure to radiation has an additive, or cumulative effect. The radiation from medical and dental X-ray are added to the natural background radiation, thus, resulting in greater total exposure.

The half lives of radioactive wastes produced by fission reactors vary widely from 0.96 second for xenon-143, to long as 24,400 years for plutonium-239. Usually at least 10 half-life periods must elapse before a source decays to a point at which it no longer constitutes a serious radiation threat. The nuclear waste must be kept in isolation to prevent human exposure. The first several hundred years are most critical. Future generations will have to watch over these wastes for centuries.

The accident of the Three Mile Island nuclear power plant at Middle Town, Pennsylvania, U.S.A. on March 28, 1979 and the Chernobyl accident in the Ukraine in the USSR on April 26, 1986 have provided sharp focus on the hazards of nuclear power.

The important environmental hazards of nuclear power are summarised below:

1. Mining of uranium-radon gas in uranium mines is a major health hazard;
2. Enrichment of fissionable uranium from 0.7 per cent to about 3 per cent;

3. Pelletization of uranium'
4. Transportation of radioactive materials;
5. Leekage of radioactive material from fuel element to receiving body through cool-out;
6. Disposal of nuclear waste material-currently about 2700 tonnes of spent nuclear fuel are stored at sixty five nuclear power plants throughout the country.
7. Human error and/ or mechanical failure internal to installation;
8. Human error and/ or mechanical failure external to installation;
9. Natural catastrophe; and
10. Malicious human activity

These and other considerations suggest that the chance a major nuclear accident may not be vanishingly small and the environmental consequences are truly serious.

Non-conventional sources of energy

The energy that conventional sources can provide is far below our present requirements. In addition, the conventional sources of energy like firewood and fossil fuel are fast shrinking. During many year in the past we have suffered form fossil fuel are fast shirking. During many years in the past we have suffered from shortages of energy mainly because the energy demand jumps ahead of its supply. Therefore, to meet the growing energy demand of the expanding population, new and renewable energy sources need to be developed. In 1982, a separate Department of Non-Convention energy sources was created by the Government of India to promote the harnessing of solar, wind, biomass, geothermal oceanic energy sources.

Solar energy

Solar energy, unlike other conventional energy sources, is received abundantly all over the country and provides a source of inexhaustible energy which is non-polluting. India is indeed fortunate to receive an abundance of sun0shine with about 164802100 Kwh/M^2/ year with 250 to 300 days of useful sun-shine a year. There are a number of possible ways to use in abundance the renewable supply of solar energy. The important among them are various types of heating devices, such as, solar coolers, solar dryers and solar heaters, which use the heating property of solar energy. solar energy can also be converted into electricity by photovoltaic systems. This is accomplished by a special silicon cell which produces electricity when exposed to sun-light. The output from one such cell is small, but a panel of silicon cells connected together produces sufficient power to run water pumps, traffic lights, radio, TV or other appliances.

Wind

Wind is a renewable source of energy and one of the earliest sources of power exploited by mankind to augment his muscle power. The windmill is an invention that sates from the earliest times of recorded history. Egyptians used windmills as early a 3600 B.C. to lift water. The use of wind energy for driving ships, lifting water grain grinding, sugarcane crushing, turning of the machines of factories, and for doing many other task developed progressively over the centuries. In the nineteenth century wind was used to generate electricity.

Although wind is ubiquitous, it varies widely from one station to another in its intensity and magnitude. It also varies diurnally and seasonally. Therefore, its potential differs drastically from one location to another. Windmills can be installed in those parts of the country where an average wind speed of 8-10 kmph prevails. Coastal areas, mountain tops, grasslands, and islands are the more favourable sites for harnessing wind power. Since wind does not blow all the time, the power output of wind turbines is highly variable and sometimes unpredictable. In India, a number of water pumping windmills have been indigenously developed. Over 1.750 pumping windmills had been installed under a demonstration project by March 1987. Five wind farms, four of 5450 K and one of 1.1 MW, installed in the costal areas, have contributed over 4.0 million units of electricity to the national grid.

The relative contribution of wind power in comparison with other energy sources is going to be small. However, this sources could make vital contributions in remote areas with favourable wind resources. The Department of Non-conventional Energy Sources has taken the initiative for wind monitoring and preparation of wind maps of different parts of the country.

Biomass

Mankind from time immemorial has been using biomass to meet the energy needs. Biomass includes, strictly speaking, all living material, whether plant or animal. Interests has focused recently on new and more efficient sources of biomass creation and improved methods or processing to retain ad much energy as possible and produce usable fuel.

Biogas

Cattle dung, human excreta and other organic wastes which have biological origin are unusable biomass and pose a grave danger to public health, if not disposed off safely. The biogas technology which has developed during the past few decades has opened up the possibility of disposing these obnoxious wastes by converting them into useful products, mainly biogas and organic manure.

A biogas plant operates in the simple principle that when cattle dung or any organic residue is fermented under anaerobic conditions or in the absence of free oxygen, a combustible gas in generated. Agricultural, domestic, human and animal wastes, water hyacinth or any other organic material can be used as feed-stock for biogas production. Distillery wastes can be suitably used for biogas generation. Obnoxious aquatic weeds, like water hyacinth, can also be used as feed-sock for biogas generation.

The gas produced by the bacterial feeding on the organic material consists of two parts of methane and one part of carbon dioxides. It is clean pollution-free fuel. It is tapped from the gas collector and can be used for cooling, lighting, pumping water, electricity generation or as fuel for any other purpose. The gas production is maintained by periodically introducing fresh dung into the digester. The spent slurry over-flown from the digester is relatively free from pathogens and is extremely suitable as organic manure or soil conditioner. In rural areas, biogas offers an excellent solution to the potential sources of environmental degradation. Organic wastes which are potential sources of environmental degradation are converted into useful products namely clean fuel and organic manuar, much needed by rural communities,

Biogas offers many indirect advantages such as conservation of forests which are being increasingly exploited for firewood by the rural communities. It can also relieve women and children from the drudgey of collecting and transporting had loads of firewood over long distances. Village sanitation can also be improved if latrines are attached to biogas plants.

China and india are world leaders in biogas technology, The central government encourages installation of biogas plants by providing cash subsides. By March 1987 over 4.8 lakh family type biogas plants were already installed in our country.

Geothermal energy

Geothermal energy, the natural heat contained within the earth is generally too deeply buried to be utilized. However, in some areas of the world that have experienced recent volcanic activity, geothermal resources may exist that can be exploited economically. These are usually found in regions of hot springs or areas where the deep hot rock is known to be fractured or to have spaces that permit water or steam to be circulated to carry heat to the surface.

At such places source for electricity generation, space heating drying and refrigeration. It is competitive with other technologies.

In our country the potential for geothermal energy has been identified as occurring in 4 regions: (1) the Non-Western Himalayas covering Ladakh. Himachal Pradesh, Punjab and Uttar Pradesh, (2) the Narmada-Sone Valley.(3) the Damodar Valley, and (4) the West Coast. Forty six hydrothermal areas have been identified where the temperature of the spring water exceeds 150C. A. 7.5 tonne capacity cold storage pilot plant based on geothermal energy has been installed at Manikaran in Himachal Pradesh as a joint venture of the Indian Institute of Technology. Delhi and the Geological Survey of India, Lucknow. Plans ark afoot to use geothermal energy at Pauge Valley, Ladakh for poultry framing and mushroom cultivation.

Ocean energy

The form of energy available from the oceans include Ocean Thermal Energy Conversion, wave energy and tidal energy. The surface layers of the oceans are continually heated by the sub-especially in the tropical belt. Enormous quantities of energy ar stored in the surface layers which have higher temperatures ranging between 24 C to 30C. However, at lower depth, 1,00 M or below, the water temperature ranges between 4 C to 10C. This temperature difference is exploited to generate electricity by a process called Ocean Thermal Energy Conversion. The technical feasibility of OTEC is well established, but the costs are high and further development work needs to be done before it is harnessed. The potential can be successfully exploited for generating electricity. The surging and receding tides produce powerful water currents in run electric turbines for electricity generation. The promising areas of the country are the Gulf of Cambay, the Gulf of Kutch and the Sunderbans.

Ocean waves contain considerable energy. The ocean surface is in a state of dynamic interaction with the wind which imparts energy to waves. The wave motion is both horizontal and vertical. The vertical movement of the wave can be harnessed by movement of a float against an anchor.

4 Social Behaviour and Population Interaction

Two behavioural phenomena which are wide-spread throughout the animal kingdom, and which have considerable significance in population ecology, are terri-torialism and dominance hierarchies. Territorialism is essentially a social pattern of spatial utilization by which individual or groups have control over certain units of space. Dominance hierarchies are an-ordered systems which determine individual access and priorities to natural resources. Both of these phenomena relate to population ecology intimately because they represent systems of behavioural control which affect the abundance and distribution of animals, their reproductive patterns and their mortality patterns. Many studies of territorial or rank oriented species have shown for example, that individuals without territory and low ranking individuals have less reproductive success and higher mortality rates than those who hold territory and/or have higher rank.

Territorialism

A territory has been defined as any area which is

defended against other member of the same species. It may be occupied and defended by an individual as in the case of a male stickleback fish (Gasterosteus aculeatus); by a pair as in the case of many birds or by a social group, as in the case of vervet monkeys (Cercopithecus aethiops) and gibbons (Hylobates lar). It may encompass most or all of the occupant's home range including his nesting and foraging areas, as in primate territories; it may include only a limited area around a nest site of feeding site, as in many birds; or it may involve only a very small plot of ground on which mating occurs, as in the Uganda kob (Adenota kob), an African antelope. Hence, territorialism is a highly variable and complex phenomenon, and involves a wide spectrum of behaviour patterns. In all cases, however the essential feature is that individual animals, or groups of animals, have controlling ownership over a given piece of property. Within this property they have the right of utilization over the space and the resources contained therein.

Territories are established and maintained by a great variety of behaviour patterns and communicative displays. Initially, the establishment of a territory may involve active aggressive behaviour and fighting. The territorial combats of siamese fighting fish, jungle fowl, elephant seals and wild antelope are well known. Those combats are often vigorous and are true tests of strength, injuries are common, and in rare cases, death may occur. Most frequently, however, the vanquished animal merely retreats and vacates the territory.

Once established territories are most often maintained by communicative signals and displays. These signals may be visual, auditory or olfactory in nature. Most fish have visual territorial displays which consist of spreading the fins and brightening the colors. Some fish have active sound production in territorial calls, as for example the Atlantic toadfish (Opsanus tau). Most birds which are territorial have a combination of vocalizations and visual displays. The male song bird of many species perches in a conspicuous spot and repeatedly gives forth his song, which serves more often as territorial threat than as a mating attraction. Mammals typically use a combination of auditory and olfactory signals as communicative displays in the maintenance of territory. Some of the arboreal primates, such as the gibbon and the howler monkey (Alouatta palliata) have an advanced vocal pattern which conveys information about the position of the group and indicates that the territory is occupied. Many carnivores, such as the wolf, lion and tiger (Felis tigris) have territorial calls which can be heard for several miles, and they also have olfactory signals in scent glands and urine which are used to mark the boundaries of territories. The scent signals may persist for days or even weeks, and thus serve as more stable cues than serve as more stable cues than vocalizations which fade rapidly.

Territorialism is common among many higher invertebrates (crustacea, insects, spiders, etc.) and throughout all vertebrate classes. Territorialism can be found in fish amphibia, reptiles, birds and mammals, which seem to operate on much the same principles and have basically the same functions. Although this is true, it must not obscure the fact that there are many animals which do not show territorialism. Many species do not stake out specific territorial claims and do not actively defend given tracts of habitat. Often one can find closely related species which are territorial in one case, and nonterritorial in another. In ungulates, for example, the Indian blackbuck (Antilope cervicapra) is territorial, whereas the Indian swamp deer (Cervus duvacelli) is not. In primates, the gibbon and the howler monkey are clearly territorial, whereas the rhesus monkey (Macaca mulatta) and the chimpanzee (Pan troglodytes) are not.

Even within the same species there are circumstances in which the individuals of some populations are territorial distributed and other circumstance in which they are not. This is true in ungulates for example, many of which are territorial during the rut or mating season, but the same individuals are non-territorial at other times of the year. Apart from this obvious correlation with breeding, however, there is evidence in some species that territorialism is related to the population density and/or environmental circumstances. In the Japanese salmon (Plecoglossus altiveli), individual fish are territorial at low population density, but as density increases, individuals give up their territories and form a school. Wild house mice (Mus musculus) show similar behaviour with territorialism at low population densities, and mass group behaviour at high population densities.

This variability is related to environmental factors and differences in social behaviour of key individuals.

In view of these facts, it does not seem warranted to consider territorialism an instinctive pattern of behaviour. Territorialism is certainly common and wide spread, but by no means universal within limited animal groups or even within a single species. It seems more appropriate to consider territorial behaviour a flexible ecological adaptation—a social and behavioural means of utilizing space.

Dominance hierarchies

Whereas territories function to allot resources on a spatial basis, dominance hierarchies allot resources on an individual priority basis within the same physical space. Hierarchical systems have been observed in all vertebrate classes and in many invertebrates.

Dominant animals have priority access to food, mates, nest sites and resting locations. Dominance is often manifested between animals by single physical displacement by the displacement of one individual by another at a feeding or resting site. Occasionally it involves displays or threats, and rarely it may involve direct fighting. The latter is more common in initial encounters in which the dominance rank or social status of each individual is not yet determined, but once established the hierarchy is then usually established by display or by social memory. Once a rhesus monkey has established high rank, it does not have to constantly display this rank in a stable social group. The high rank of some individuals and low rank of other become an accepted social norm within the group. Only when the situation becomes unstable through death, emigration or invasion does there have to be an avert re-establishment of rank within a dominance hierarchy.

So far as we have seen territorialism and dominance hierarchies as two types social systems which play a regulatory role in population dynamics, the first by regulating of space second by controlling individual priorities within a common space. In some animal species and populations, territorialism and dominance hierarchies apparently serve as sensitive feedback mechanisms which influence dispersal, mortality reproductive success and population size. In other species and circumstances, territorialism and hierarchical structures are often subject to breakdown and collapse. Ecological consequences are then profound and extensive. In many rodent populations, excessive population growth and crowding is often associated with the following phenomena: a breakdown of stable territoria-lism and dominance structure, reduced fertility as evidence by lowered pregnancy rates, high prenatal loss and low infant survival, poor nest construction and poor maintenance, nest fouling and pollution, high aggression and wounding deteriorating health in the majority of the population, abnormal aggregations of individuals in the 'behavioural sink' pattern and finally population decline.

Social behaviour in population regulation

The detailed study to territorilism and dominance

hierachies is really in the realm of ethology and animal behaviour, but the functions and consequences of these behavioural systems have a great deal of ecological significance. It has been abundantly demonstrated in many territorial animals that the holders of territory have the greatest breeding success. In fact, in some animals, non-territorial animals usually fail to breed.

Similarly in those social groups characterized by dominance hierarchies the high ranking animals have the greatest breeding success and the low ranking members have less success or fail entirely in breeding efforts. In chicken flocks, low ranking roosters show frequent counting behaviour, sometimes more than dominant rooster, but they have relatively little success in completing copulations.

It thus seems clear that the social systems of territorialism and dominance hierarchies have a limiting function in population dynamics; that is, they limit the breeding to those individuals which are ecologically and behaviorally most successful in establishing territory or high rank. Theoretically, as population densities increase, and space becomes more limited, a smaller proportion of individuals within the population is able to achieve territories or high rank, and thus total reproduction is reduced in relation to population size. Ideally, these behaviors are density-dependent population limiting factors; that is, the higher the density, the greater the limiting effect on the population.

The role of social behavior in population regulations has been discussed at great length by

Wynne-Edwards. Wynne-Edwards proposed that the basic long-term population level of many animals is established by food and resource availability, but that social behaviour establishes a more immediate regulating influence on population size and density. This influence on social behaviour, he felt, comes into play before critical population levels are achieved; that is, before starvation and/or damaging violent aggression are conspicuous.

Thus, according to Wynne-Edwards most animals have intrinsic, self-regulatory population mechanisms which operate via social and behavioural feedback systems. These social and behavioral feedbacks are usually ritualized displays which relate to territorialism and dominance hierarchies, and thus convey information about population density. Therefore, regulatory feedback is provided according to the intensity of social competition. In other words, ritualized displays, or conventionalized rivalries, regulated breeding success and thus population numbers.

Wynne-Edwards provides numerous examples of this hypothesis, including the complex display patterns of gallinaceous birds, (prairie chickens, sharp-tailed grouse, peacocks, bower birds et al.) waterfowl and many song birds. He also considers the vocal choruses of amphibians, the schooling of fish, and the flocking and birds and mammals as examples of complex social behaviour which serve the function of conveying information about population density and social competition.

Many aspects of Wynne-Edwards' theory are controversial especially when he theorized that most social behaviour has actually evolved as a means of controlling population levels. Wynne-Edwards proposed, for example, that territorialism has arisen as a social means of preventing over population. This theory has met substantial criticism from other ecologists and students of behaviour. These authors felt that there is little reliable evidence to support this hypothesis even though it is logically very attractive. Brown pointed out that, "Population regulation is never completely under the control of the species by itself, but depends in a complex way on interactions between members of the ecological community." Thus, Brown felt one must consider the interaction of all factors, including predation, disease, food supply, interspecific dynamics of any given species. Brown found satisfactory evidence that territorialism tends to space individuals over available habitat, that it increases emigration and morality rates in individuals unsuccessful in finding territories, and that it has arisen in response to individual selection resulting from aggressive competition.

The more detailed aspects of this controversy are out side the scope of introductory ecology. On the more basic parts of the hypotheses—namely, that social behaviour provides some regulatory feedback on population ecology—there is certainly no question that this is true in most animal populations.

Even this concession must not obscure the fact, however, that some animals have such poorly developed and/or variable responses to increased density and crowding that they can readily breed themselves into starvation or conditions of violent aggression and extreme social strife. White-tailed deer populations, for example have frequently increased to the point of extensive starvation. Lemming and other rodent populations have also increased to the point of mass behavioral strife where social mortality becomes extensive.

Quite probably, some human populations are also in this category, providing example of populations in which social feedback limiting population growth often does not into operation until the point of starvation arrives (as in China and India), or until the point of violent and destruction aggression breaks forth (as in many wards in which population pressure has had a causative influence) or until social morality becomes limiting (as in countries where abortion is a significant form of population regulation).

It is scientifically important to consider animal population in which environmental crises and/or behavioural breakdowns occur. In terms of human value judgments these seem to be cases of population regulation by wasteful and sometimes tragic means. In evolutionary terms, however, many of the populations showing these phenomena are of highly exploitative natures, meet new environmentral situations had expand into available opportunities. Perhaps their lack of frigid, stereotyped behaviour and ecology, and their lack of precisely tuned population feedback systems, enables them to seize each new ecologic opportunity to the fullest extent.

Some of the best examples of such species are the domestic rodents especially the wild house mouse, the wild Norway rat (Pattus norvegious) and the Asian bandicoot rat (Bandicota bengalensis). Numerous ecological studies over the last 25 years have shown these species to have the following population characteristics:

1. They have tremendous reproductive potential and under certain environmental circumstances they often show invasive and eruptive population behaviour.
2. Populations can readily exceed the carrying capacity of the environment and this can result in sudden population decline.
3. Populations fluctuate widely, natural control is often abrupt and "ecologically wasteful", in terms of individual health and welfare.
4. Population regulation often involves social disruption and destructive behaviour.

These characteristics have been observed frequently in both natural and artificial populations of rodents over the past 40 years. The natural social behaviour of the Norway rat and wild house mouse includes both territorial and hierarchical behaviour. Females tend to the territorial around the nest site so that they normally exclude adult males and strange females. Often two of three females nest together in a communal agreement. Males are also territorial if population density is not excessively high, and high ranking males defend a system of runway and the females living therein. The size and patterning of the territories depend upon the rank of the male, the density and social structure of the population and the nature of the habitat.

In a stable habitat both population levels and social structures of domestic rats might remain quite stable over a period of time. But the habitats of domestic rodents are characteristically unstable with changing amounts of food (around farm, for example where harvests and food stores come and go), changing mortality patterns (as control compaigns) or disease outbreaks wax and wane) or changing cover conditions(as trash availability rises and falls) so that the populations are often experiencing drastically changing resource conditions. Under these circumstances, the populations respond rapidly with surges or declines of growth.

Under periods of rapid population growth leading to high densities, a variety of phenomena have been observed. There is often rapidly increasing social contact resulting in an increase in aggressive interactions. This frequently lead to a breakdown of territorial boundaries, increased crowding of the nest sites and sharply increased mortality of young nests become trampled and destroyed. Females often desert the nests or actually kill the young. Wounds become frequent, especially an adult males forming sites for mites to invade the skin, so that acarine dermatits may achieve epidemic proportions.

With a breakdown of territorial behaviour, bizarre aggregations developed so that clusters of individuals all in poor physical states appeared. Calhoun referred to such aggregations as "behavioral sinks". They are self-stimulating aggregations of individuals often collectively showing abnormal behaviour patterns. Some individuals become inactive and socially withdrawn. As these conditions progress only limited portions of the environment are utilized but these become excessively polluted. Thus, the stage is set for both high social mortality and high disease mortality and population often collapses as rapidly as it built up. After the crash if the environment recovers the surviving individuals recuperate and population growth may begin again.

The detailed of this theme differ considerably in different studies and different species. In come circumstances, there may be a cessation of production so that no young are born into the crowded population, as occurred in house mouse populations studied by Crowcroft and Row. In other circumstances reproduction may continue, but there may be massive infant mortality of all young born. In still other cases, crowding may stimulate excessive migration and disposal as in lemmings and these mass migrations are often accompanied or determinated by high mortality.

In all cases, a similar syndrome prevails. There is usually a drastic change in social organization and behaviour which most often have a major influence on reproduction and mortality. In domestic rodents these changes characteristically involve a breakdown in social stability and a disruption of normal territorial, reproductive and parental behaviour. Frequently parinatal processes are most dramatically affected, so that this pre-and postnatal survival of the young is reduced.

Population interaction

All population of living organism exist in a network of interactions with other population. Many of these interactions are subtle and complex than direct food relationships. Others are competitive or limiting to the interacting populations. The degree of intimacy in the relationships of thc organism inhabiting a particular habitat varies greatly. These association may be either beneficial or harmful to both the patterns or beneficial to one partner and harmful to the other. If the relationship is beneficial either to one or both partners, it is called 'Positive Interaction' or cooperation. This may be interaspecific (Ex. Social life of inspects) or Inter specific (Ex: Commensalism, Mutualism & Symbiosis). The interrelations between individuals that are harmful to one or more of the participants is called Negative interaction. It includes "Parasitism, Predation and Competition".

Commensalims

The term 'Commensalism' was first proposed by Van-Benedan (1876) to the animals that share the same food.

"Two or more animals that live together and do not enter into any kind of Physiological Union are referred to as `Commensals' and this association is called as `Commensalism! The relation is unequal in that only one individual gets the benefit from the association while the other is neither benefited nor injured. The Chief benefits from this association are (i) Shelter, (ii) Anchorage (iii) Transportation and (iv) The food supply.

Types of commensals:

A commensal which attaches or lives upon the host's body is called as 'ectocommensal'. If a commensal lives within the body of the host in the respiratory or alimentary tract or in any other body cavity which opens to outside, is referred to as endocommensal.

Vorticella, a Protozoan animal is an ectocommensal which is attached to the legs of the freshwater shrimp (prawn like) by slender stalks. The 'Sucker fish' is another ectocommensal which attaches itself to the body of shark, or sword fish or seaturtle with the help of its sucker. All the ectocommensals are small in size and not burdensome to the host.

The harmless protozoans in the intenstinal tract of mammals and micro-organisms in the canal system of sponges are the examples of an ectocommensals!.

An example of commensalism is the remora-shark relationship where the remora fish (Echenesis naucrates) attaches to the skin of the shark by means of a strange sucker disc and transported widely and rapidly by the shark's motive power. The remora also consumes food remnants cast off from the jaws of the shark. Thus the remora benefits in two ways from this attachment and the shark is relatively unaffected although its swimming speed may be slightly impeded.

Many large organisms provide commensal harborage for other organisms externally and internally. Large tropical trees provide habits for numerous commensal plants and animals. Trunks and branches provide attachment sites for epiphytes such as orchids, and recesses between buttress roots provide attachment harborage for bats tree frogs, lizards, insects and many other organisms. Whales provide attachment sites for barnacles, algae, and other sessile marine forms. These plants and animals are not parasitic, that is, they do not extract nutrients from the habitat provided by the host.

Most animals, including man, also contain internal commensals. The human digestive tract is inhabited by several types of bacteria and protozoa such as Entamobea cole, which are neither parasitic not pathogenic, but merely residual in the alimentary canal.

Another common type of commensalism occurs when various species of plants and animals use burrows or nests constructed by another species. Termite nests provide ecologic niches for more than 100 species of other animals including ants, aphids, beetles millipedes and isopod crustaceans. Tube-dwelling annelids of the genus Chaetopterus which inhabit the tidal zone of the seashore provide habitats for small crabs of the genus Polyonyx. The crab benefits by the protection of the tube, and it apparently does no harm to the annelid worm which originally built the tube.

Commensalism may be obligatory, in which one organism depends entirely on another for its habitat or it may be facultative in which each organism may be independent but one is enhanced in the presence of the other. An example of obligatory commensalism is the relationship between the algae, Basicladia, and certain freshwater turtles. The algae grows only on the backs of the turtle. Similarly the bivalve mollusc Ostrea grows almost exclusively on the roots of the red mangrove off the coast of Florida. Attached to the shell of the horse-shoe crab, Limulus, are several species of molluscs, barnacles and annelid worms which again are not parasitic but only residential and some of them live only on the Limulus shell. The oyster crab is a small crustacean which lives only in the mantle cavity is a small crustacean which lives only in the mantle cavity of oysters. These all represent cases in which one species of plant or animals has evolved a dependent relationship does not involve feeding upon the tissues of the host. The possibility exists that this is one evolutionary route toward parasitism and the distinction between obligatory commensalism and parasitism is often difficult to draw.

Facultative commensalism is represented by the relationship between the borrowing owl (Speotyto cuniculario) and the prairie dog (Cynomys sp.) The burrowing owl often nests in prairie dog burrows but is not confined to such burrows. In the north polar regions, the arctic fox Clo pex lagopus) feeds in the winter time on the remains of seals killed by polar bears (Thalarctos maritimus) though it may have other sources of food as well. Probably the majority of commensal relationship are facultative.

It is especially interesting to consider animal populations which form facultative commensal relationships with men. Among vertebrates perhaps the best examples are domestic rodents such as house mice and Norway rats which have increased in abundance and distribution by their association with human habitation and agriculture. The house sparrow, pigeon and Asian house crow and Asian house shrew or musk shrew have also greatly increased their population sizes through human associations. Cities, towns and farms provide increased food supplies and nesting sites of these animals. The rhesus monkey in India is one of the few primates which has become a facultative commensal of man. The rhesus can readily survive in forests without man, but it becomes especially abundant around villages and towns of the Gangetic basin where it could live on agricultural produce.

Some more examples among the inverterbrates are as follows:-

(1) The peacrabs are found living in the mouth cavity of bivalves. They steal food collected by the host and do not cause any injury.

(2) A number of micro organism live as commensals in the canal system of sponges.

(3) Polynoid polychaetes are found in the pallial chambers of gastropods and in the ambulacral groves of star fishes.

(4) A host of commensals such as worms, Brittlestars, molluscs, little fishes, prawns-crabs etc. are found among the coral reefs.

(5) Small pelagic fishes live under the umbrellar shelter of large jelly fishes.

(6) Some fishes live in the borrows of worms and crustaceans.
(7) A number of copepeds live within the Ascidiann or Sea anemones.
(8) Barnacles attach on the skin of whales or back of turtles.

In all these associations one of the partners which is generally smaller derives benefits of anchorage, shelter, food and transportation.

Mutualism

Mutualism is an association between two or more animals in which all derive mutual benefit with no harm to any of the partners. "Symbiosis" term also often used to this type of relationship (Properly refers to the intimate associations to two or more dissimilar organisms).

Mutualism may be seen between animals and plants and between animals and other animals.

Ist Type : Mutualism between Plants and Animals

This association is important to the reproduction of many kinds of plant species. Plants attract insects by their sweet, nectar or colour. The insects visit plants to get their food. The plants dust them with pollen and the insects carry the pollen from flower to flower.

In the distribution of seeds, plants take the help of animals. Plants provide fruits and seeds pass in their hard coat, undigested through the alimentary canal of the animal and are distributed in its droppings.

For instance a species of Alacia grows little

pearshaped masses of food for the ants, and hollow thrones (Myrmecolphilous stipules) in which the ants take shelter. In turn the ants defend the plant from the attack of other insects.

2nd Type: Mutualism between Animals and other Animals

Birds display this type of relationship. The cow bird and Bison, the Oxpecker and the antelope, crow and the cattle exhibit mutualistic relationship.

In all these associations the birds render considerable service to their hosts by ridding them of ticks and external parasites and also serves as sentinels. In turn the birds receive a constant food supply.

An interesting example is between a 'Crocodile' and the bird (Pluvianus aegyptius). The bird removes leeches and fragments of food in decaying condition of the crocodile. The crocodile opens its jaws and permits the search then finally the bird receives the food from the crocodile.

The common starling bird may also perform the same function from the sheep.

The association of ostriches and Zaebras is also said to be of mutual benefit.

Birds and Insects

Birds have also developed relationship with insects for mutual benefit. The horn bill of Africa harbours a number of insects in its nest. The female horn bill will be confined to the nest at the time of egg laying and breeding. The male bird feeds her with fruits.

Various ants plants (Lice Aphids) are associated as Commensals.

The most common Commensals among marine forms are the Hydroids and Sea anemones found on the shell of Hermit crab. In this association both of them are benefited.

The Indian Rock (Mincus inermic services as a moving home to zoophytes small polyps are encrusted on this fish.

In this relationship the fishes obtain protection from predators and they pay for it by luring large fishes within the range of tentacles.

The relationship between *Hermit Crab* and *Sea anemone* is very interesting. Here the Crab obtains protection from predatory fish by the shrinking power of sea anemone. The sea anemone also gets an advantage of transportation of feeding grounds and gets food fragments when the crab captures and eats another animal.

Sponges growing on the shell of Hermit Crab protect it by producing bad odour. Here the advantages to the sponge is that it is carried to new waters for its own food.

Thus, the mutualistic relationships between plants and animals, and animals and other animals prove to be beneficial mutually and reciprocally to the participants.

Like commensalism, mutualism may be obligatory or faculative. An example of obligatory mutualism is provided by the relationship between the flagellate protozoan Trichonympha, and woodeating termites. These species cannot live without each other. The protozoan lives only in the digestive tract of the termite. The stomach and caecum of the horse contains millions of ciliate protozoa and bacteria which digest cellulose for the horse and provide 20 per cent of its nitrogen requirement per day. These intestinal microorganisms are essential for the normal growth and health of the horse.

An elaborate form of obligatory mutualism occurs between some ants (e.g., Cremastogaster lineolata) and aphids or plant lice (e.g. Aphis caliginosa). The ants maintain the aphids in specially constructed nests, and they feed upon a nutrient liquid secreted by the aphids. The aphids have sometimes been called "cows" because they release the secretion when stroked by the antennae of the ants. Thus the ants receive food from ants. Many other anthropods, including mites, springtails, flies, wasps and beetles, have developed similar complex relationships are based on interspecific communication systems through which the different species jointly utilize food, shelter of other resources.

Many mutualistic relationships are facultative; that is, both populations can exist without the other, but both are favoured when living together. Baboons and impalas, for example, can survive well without each other, but each provides a unique protective warning system for the other when they live in association. Squirrels facilitate the extension and propagation of hickory trees by buying the nuts, but the hickory trees can propogate without squirrels and the squirrels can likewise survive without hickory nuts, if an adequate supply of other food is available.

Man has capitalized on mutualism as a biological principle in the development of agriculture. The domestication of plants and animals originated in facultative commensalism or mutualism. At the down of agriculture, 10,000 years ago, man could live without domesticated plants and animals, but as he developed these relationships then evolved into obligatory commensalism and mutualism. Modern man obviously cannot live without the domesticated plants and animals of agriculture, and many of these domesticated forms cannot live without the special husbandry provided by man.

Symbiosis

The term Symbiosis was first coined by DeBray in 1879. It means "living together."

"Symbiosis is an association between two or more organisms that live together in close physiological union for the mutual benefit." Here the term Symbiosis refers to the intimate association of two or more dissimilar organism. One of the partners may be known as Symbiont.

Symbiosis offers from commensalism and mutualism in two important respects.

(1) The relation between two partner is much more intimate in Symbiosis than in other relations.
(2) It is mostly obligatory.

Symbiotic associations are known to occur between plants and other plants, animals and plants; and animals and other organisms.

First type symbiotic association among plants

This type of associations is demonstrated in (i) Fungi and algue which form lichens; (ii) Fungal mycorrhizae and the roots of many flowering plants and (iii) Nitrogen fixing bacteria and the roots of legumes. In all these associations, there is metabolic interdependence. In the lichens, algae produces food and fungi provide mineral and protection. The intimate association between the roots of flowering plants and mycorrhizae results in the formation of a composite fungus-roots structure which differs from the roots without mycorrhizae. Here the fungi require soluble carbohydrates and substances and they get them from root secretions. Here also the association is intimate the benefits are mutual.

The importance of the Nitrogen-fixing bacteria (Rhizobia associated with legumes is well known. Legumes posses on their rootlets, a number of swellings, inhabited by the bacteria. Here, they derive carbohydrates from the host and in turn they fix the atmospheric nitrogen in the roots. This "Nitrogen" is used by the plants.

This is clearly a beneficial partnership.

Second type: Symbiotic-Associations between plants and animals

The most notable symbiotic association between plants and animals occur between freshwater coelenterate (Chlorohydra Viridissina) and an algae. In this association the animal obtains Carbohydrates and a supply of Oxygen evolved as a result of Photosynthesis by the algae. The large in turn receive protection and Dioxide for photosynthesis released by the animal during respiration.

Hydra and Algae relationship is also one of the good examples. The mutual benefits of hydra an algae are

Chlorachydra (animal)	*Zoochlorellae (Plant)*
i) It gives phosphorus and nitrogen compounds for protein formation.	i) Plants gives Oxygen
ii) It gives Carbon dioxide for the pho' synthesis in plants.	ii) Excretory materials.
iii) It gives protection to algae (Plant)	iii) Carbon dioxide (from respiration)

Planeria and an animal algae and a plant symbiotic association is also a good example. Here the symbiotic benefits are same as in coelenterate and algae. Here, the presence of algae is indispensable for the worm and this is obligatory.

Association between fungus and insects

The wood boring beetles have an elaborate apparatus on the head for carrying the Fungus. Others carry Fungus in the midgust to be regurgitated for cultivation. The females of this species have an apparatus connected with evipositor which coat their eggs with fungal spores as they are laid. In all these associations, the Fungus provide food and shelter, and it grows on the excretory material of its host.

Third Type: Symbiotic Association Between Animals (Metazoa) and Microorganisms

Symbiotic associations are also seen between Metazoa and Micro-organisms many Wood-eating-insects especially termites harbour numerous protozoans in their alimentary canal. It has been shown that the gut of termites can live on a nitrogen-free diet so long as protozoa are present. This suggests that they may be capable of nitrogen fixation of the synthesis of protein from carbohydrates. Here the protozoans produce specific enzymes "Cellulose," and "Cellobiase," which are responsible for cellulose digestion.

Similar association is seen in the gut of Cockroach, "Cryptocersus." In all these cases the protozoan gets shelter and food.

Mammals and Bacteria

In this association symbolic bacteria are present in the Caecum of rabbits and rumen of cattle. Here, the bacteria utilize the inorganic nitrogen and sulphates for the synthesis of essential amino acids, which can't be synthesized by the animal. In turn to mammals, the Bacteria produce Vitamin B12 (in ruminants). In man also some of the vitamins are produced by the intestinal Bacteria.

The Symbolic Bacteria are also present in the gut of the South African Honey Guide." Here, the Bacteria feeds on the Wax of honey comb the bacteria digest the Wax and gets shelter and food from the host.

Predation

In this relationship one animal is killed and eaten by another, the predator so predator is a free living animal. It is usually larger than prey. The herbivores that feed on the plant material completely are called as Plant Predators.

There are, many kinds of predation which are not necessarily so selective. The swallow feeding on moths and midges, the top minnow or trout feeding on mosquitoes, and the ant eater feeding on an ant nest is less discriminate in taking individuals. Certainly, many able and healthy individuals are preyed upon. In cases such as these, which involve large numbers, the prey population often shows great productivity which can accommodate this mass mortality. Many fish, insects, and other Invertebrates have tremendous production of eggs and larvae, but only a small percentage of these serve the onslaughts of predation and other forms of loss. For example, the horse shoe crab or Limulus of estuarine and evastal waters deposits its eggs on sandy beaches wehere they are consumed in great numbers by flocks of laughing gulls and other shore-birds. Large number of eggs also wash out to sea and are eaten by fish, whereas others are pushed up on the beach and dry out. Despite this fantastic loss of eggs and young larvae, Limulus continues to survive in large populations and has done so for the last 180 million years. It is one of the oldest animals on earth in terms of its evolutionary history, having outlived trilobites and dinosaurs by millions of years, and it is still incredibly abundant.

There has been considerable interest in predation as a factor in quantitative population control as well as its role in quality control. On one hand, sportsmen have wanted to limit predation, being concerned that predators may take excessive numbers of game birds and wildlife. Some sportsmen's organizations have therefore supported predator control campaigns against hawks, owls, foxes, coyotes, wolves, cougar and other predators in the name of conservation. On the other hand, ecologists have often been interested in promoting predation as a method of biological control of pest animals, particularly insects and rodents, and even as a necessary biological control of desirable animals such as deer, or prevent them from becoming pests.

There are also examples from the entomological literature where predation serves as a significant population control on an animal population. In a classic study of natural population balance in the knapweed galifly (Urophora jaceana), a small dipteran insect, Varley concluded that one of the major controlling factors was the predation of mince upon insect pupae. His data showed that 22 to 43 percent of the fly morality was attributable to this predation. One study of tsetse flies (Glossing spp.) in Africa, found predatory spiders to be a controlling factor on the abundance and distribution of the flies. Insect predators have also been used in applied biological control of agricultural pests in a few cases. In California, the cottony cushion scale, an hemiptoran insect pest of citrus crops, was effectively controlled by a predatory ladybird bettle imported from Australia. In Hawaii, the sugarcane leaf hopper has been controlled by the capsid bug.

Another important aspect of predation as an influence in population ecology and natural selection is the great variety of adaptations which have arisen in response to it. Protective coloration, warning coloration and mimicry fall into this category. Also, the morphological and behaviour, freezing behaviour and many other specialized patterns have developed in various species as adaptations to reduce mortality through predation. One particularly interesting system which has been studied in some detail is the intimate relationship between certain moths and the bats which prey upon them. The bats locate the moths by emitting ultrasonic pulses and detecting reflecting echoes flying moths, a natural sonar system (Novick, 1969). The moths have evolved the ability to detect these ultrasonic pulses of the bats, and upon perceiving the approach of a feeding bat, they instantly go into complicatd diversionary flight spirals to avoid the bat. The introduction becomes on serial "dog flight" between bat and moth, with the moth trying to avoid the bat. This ability and behaviour has evolved in selective response to predation in the same way that cryptic coloration has evolved. In both case the advantageous mutations have been selected and propagated.

Parasitism

"Parasitism" is the relation between two individuals, wherein the parasite receives benefit at the expense of the host, therefore, parasitism is form of disoperation.

In this association, the parasite receives (i) food (ii) shelter (iii) and protection, at the expense of the host. The host does not derive any benefit from the relationship. A parasite does not ordinarily kill its host atleast not until the parasite completes its reproductive cycle.

Classification

Parasites are classified into different categories

depending upon their relation with the host.

1. Temporary Parasites

The animals which spend only a part of their life cycle as parasites are called temporary parasites."

For Example; The glochidium (is a Larva of freshwater mussel) leads a parasitic life.

It attaches itself the skin of fish with the help of hooks present on the shell and later it is covered by the skin of fish. It remains burried thus for several weeks and emerges as young animals to lead a free life.

Example 2. In prasitic Hymenoptera, the eggs are deposited into the body of another insect (Caterpillar), where the entire larvae stage is spent the larva feeds on the fat body of the host. Until it attains pupal stage. Finally it emerges as an adult and leads a free living life.

2. Permanent Parasites

Some parasites have continuous association with their hosts, they are called permanent parasites. They spend their entire life as parasites.

For example: Trichinea worm, Malarial Parasite etc.,

Permanent prarasites often found among lower animals. They almost always require a succession of hosts or intermediat host.

3. Facultative Parasites

These are parasites (animals) which are parasitic only when there is a change for parasitic life, leading free life otherwise.

Eg: Meggocs of some flies, Lamprey etc.,

4. Obligatory Parasite

Some species are forced to lead a Parasitic life. If not, they can't live. This type of parasites are called obligatory parasites.

Eg: Filarial Wornm Cestodes etc.,

5. External Parasites

Those which live outside the body of the host are called external parasites. Eg. Flea on birds and mammals, blood sucking lice and fleas, mites, ticks and leeches.

6. Endoparasites

These are parasites which live in the elementary tract body cavities, various organs, blood or other tissue of the host. The association between 'endoparasites' and their hosts is invariably more inntimate than that between extoparasites and hosts.

Tricchomonad flagellates, Opalnid ciliates Sporozoans, Nematodes, Cestodes and some Copepods are some of the endoparasitic forms.

The endo-parasites are further divided into 2 types based upon their exact location inside the most body.

(i) Intracellular Parasites Ex:- Plasmodium (living within the cell)

(ii) Intercellular Parasites Ex:- Tryponasome (living be tween the cells in the intercellualar spaces).

Evolution of paraitism

The origin of parasitic life in amimals is associated with attempts to secure food for themselves or their offspring. The ancestors of ecto-parasites were clearly free living forms. A free living organism could accidentally have settled on the body of a larger species where coditions were favourable for survival. For example: The biting lice might have evolved from the insects that live beneath the bark of trees. Endoparasites might have evolved from ectoparasites or directly from free-living ancestors.

Modifications and adaptations

1. *Organs of attachment:* The rasping mouth of the Lampern, and the head of tape worm equipped with 'Suckers' and 'Hooks' for attachment to the hosts gutwall are the typical examples. Among parasitic arthropods such as mites other insects claws are well developed used to cling on the external surface of the host.

2. *Body Shape:* The intestinal parasites such as the tape worm and Round worm have elongated bodies. The liver fluke have leaf-like bodies and elongated form of blood flukes are good example of this type. These arrangements are useful to suit the environment in which the parasite lives.

3. *Cuticles:* Ex: Tape worm.

Intestinal parasites face the problem of withstanding the action of the digestive juices of the host. To avoid this these parasities develop thick cuticle, offers resistance against the action of the digestive juices.

4. *Loss of Locomotary Organs:*

Ex: The fleas or Lice.

Most of the endoparasites have lost their Locomotary organs, as they are not needed. There is no need in search of food, as they have always plentiful supply of food. So the locomotary organs of the parasites disappear or differentiate into organs of attachment.

The fleas or lice (Parasitic Insects) have lost their wings, which live among the hair and feathers.

5. Digestive System:

In the tape worm, which lives in the alimentary canal of the hot, has lost its alimentary canal and absorbs already digested food from the surrounding medium. The mouth parts of the blood sucking insects have developed 'Piercing and Sucking' apparatus.

6. Loss of Sense Organs:

As the internal environment of the host is more or less uniform, there is no use of the sense organs among the endoparasites are provided only with tango receptors.

7. Complicated Reproduction:

Ex: Flat Worm, Round Worm, etc.

The reproductive function in most parasites has undergone considerable complication. It is the goal of all the functions of the organism. The endoparasites are characterized by enormous fertility.

For example (i) the human round worm lay (Ascaris Lumbricoides) eggs at a rate of 1500 a day (ii) the termatodes and cestodes lay eggs continuously (iii) Taenia solium (Tape Worm) lay eggs annually and have been estimated at 80 million (per year).

The most remarkable feature of flat Worm parasities is the presence of 'complicated reproduction'.

The effect of "Parasitism" on the host is usually harmful. The endoprasites causes effects, more marked than those by extoparasites.

The following Pathological effects caused by parasites in their hosts.

(1) The destruction of cells and tissues of the host by the parasite's movement or feeding act.

Ex: Entamoeba histolytica-eats the tissue cells of colon and red blood cells of the host, and plasmodium feeds on liver cells and erythrocytes (R.B.C.)

(2) Parasites may cause 'enlargements's and disorders of lymph glands, and liver.

Ex: Leishmania.

(3) Parasites may cause 'Malaria', (Plasmodium parasite) and 'Trypanosoma gambiense' diseases due to the secretion of toxins (Poisonous).

(4) The effects of endparasites may also be mechanical. Ex: Ascaris, is a good example when these parasites multiply in greater number they block the intestine, preventing the feree flow of food, which leads to the death of the host.

(5) The most remarkable effects of prasitism on the sexual characters are seen among crustaceans. The presence of sacculina bring spectacular changes in its host (Crab), which may result finally in death (due to the parasitic castration).

Hyperparasites:
Sometimes a parasite harbors a number of parasites in its body. They are called 'Hyperparasites'.

A typical example is, small mammal ones as 'Mouse' which invariably harbours a no of ectoparasitic fleas, which themselves contain endoparasites (Protozoans) in their alimentary Canal.

Parthenogenic and non parthenogenic parasites:
The parasite which do not cause any injury to the host are called 'Non parthenogenic parasite'. The parasite which cause disease is known as "Parthenogenic Parasite".

In man's digestive system 'Bacteria' are helpful in synthesizing' Vitamins, used to man. Some Bacteria causes numerous diseases as pneumonia, tuberculosis, diptheria, bubonic plague, cholera, syphilis and wooping cough etc.

Viruses causes, small pox, polio, yellow fever etc. Animal-like microbes causes malaria, (Plasmodium) sleeeping sickness (Trypanosona gambiense) and dysentery (Entamoeba histolytica).

Parasitism is virtually universal in all plants and animals in vertebrate animals, endoparasites are found within many of the major organ systems of the body, most commonly in the digestive, circulatory, respiratory and urogenitial systems. Ectoparasites occur on or within the skin and its appendages, such as hair scales. Throughout most of the world, man is beset with many parasitic organisms including intestinal worms (tape-worms, flukes, roundworms, etc.), intestinal protozoa (amoeba, ciliates and flagelates), parasites of the blood (microfilaria, malaria protozoa, etc.), and a variety of extoparasites (Mice, mites, ticks, mosquitoes, etc.). Many infectious microorganisms including bacteria and viruses are also parasites in the sense that they extract nutrients from the host. Some of these are pathogenic, that is, they impart the health and normal functioning of the host, as for example, the bacterial organisms of the genus shigella which cause bacillary dysentery. Others, such as some intestinal flagellates, are nonpathogenic and do not harm the host. Many parasitic organisms may be pathogenic in one individual and nonpathogenic in another. For example, most individuals, infected with Entamoeba histolytica in the digestive tract do not have amoebic dysentery, and, in fact, may have no disease symptoms at all, but in other individuals, the same organism may produce severe disease and even death. This is a matter of individual ecology and immunology which is not well understood.

As mentioned previously in the selection on communalism, theere is no sharp line of distinction between obligatory commensalism and parasitism. Theoretically, Entamoeba histolytica feeding on tissues of the host is a parasite, whereas the flagellate Trichomores hominis, feeding on digested foods before incorporation into host tissue is not a parasite, nor is Entamoeba coli feeding on undigested particles of food and intestinal bacterias.

Neither is there a sharp line of distinction between a parasite and a predator. Houseflies and vampire bats bite and suck blood form livestock, and they might be considered either parasites or predators. Normally, we think of predators as killing their prey in a short time. Man's relation to the cow is predatory when he kills it for beef, but it is parasitic when he milks it for dairy products. There are some relationships, however, in which the distinction is arbitrary, as for example, in the lamprey feeding on a host fish. The lamprey may kill the fish in a few days or a few weeks, depending upon its size in relation to the fish, and may be considered either a predator or a prasite.

Ecologically, one of the most interesting questions about parasitism is the effect of the parasite population upon the host population. The oldest and best adapted parasites have little or no pathogenic effect upon the host. Pinworm infections in children are relatively harmless, though they may cause a minor irritation around the anus. In West Bengal, studies have shown that over 75 percent of the local population harbors hookworm (Necator sp. and Ancylostoma sp.), but there is no demonstrable pathology or effect on the people. The infectious burden (i.e., the number of parasites per person) seems to be small and insignificant. Most wild animals have parasites are able to maintian excellent health with these parasites. Zebras in Kenya are intensively infected with many internal and external parasites, but they are usually in remarkably robust health.

On the other hand, there are numerous examples where parasitic infections are harmful and debiliting to the host. Certainly, hookworm necator americana in the southern United States, as it occurred 50 years ago, was a debilitating disease, sapping the strength and health of the infected person. Throughout the world, malaria still remains as a major health problem and it causes a great amount of illness and human misery. One of the most important debilitating disease of modern times is schistosomiasis an infection of blood flukes of the genus Shistosoma. This is a waterborne infection and has spread throughout the tropical world with the expansion of irrigated agriculture.

In animal populations, parasites may also weaken infected individuals. In the bighorn sheep of Wyoming and Idaho, lungworm infections are still a major cause of illness and mortality. In dogs and wolves, heartworms reduce the animal's vitality and hunting succss. In meadow vole populations, botfly parasitism causes larger spleen weights in infected mice and reduces their survival when exposed to cold temperatures. Periodic reductions of field voles in Wales have attributed in some years to heavy infections with tuberculosis among the mice, but in other years similar reductions occurred without the infection. Similarly, reductions in populations of red grouse in Scotland have been attributed in some years to the round worm parasite, Trichastrongylosus pergracilis, but this has not a consistent finding in all year. Occasional heavy mortality of gray squirrels in Baltimore has been associated with coccidiosis, caused by a protozoan parasite of the digestive tract. In 1971 a virus disease of wildfowl decimated 90 percent of the pheasants of England, in much the same way as myxomatosis reduced rabbit populations of England, and Europe in the 1950's. Thus, parasitism as an interspecific population relationship may be balanced or unbalanced in regard to its effect upon the host. A seriously unbalanced relationship, in which the host dies is, of course, selectively disadvantageous to the parasite as well.

Another outstanding feature of parasitism is the interspecific complexity which was evolved in some species. Many parasites have primary and secondary hosts and, in some cases, tertiary hosts for various stages of the life cycle. The malaria organism Plasmodium falciparum, for example has parts of its life cycle, the sexual phase of reproduction, within the mosquito, and part, the sexual phase of reproduction within the human host. Schistosomes infect man or other vertebrate animals as the primary host for sexual reproduction. The Chinese liver fluke, Clonorchis sinensis, infects man as a primary host, aquatic snails as a secondary host, and fresh-water fish as tertiary hosts. Despite the complexity of this life cycle, it is a very successful and widespread parasite, infecting millions of people throughout the Orient.

Competition

The word "competition" denotes striving for the same thing. At the ecological level competition becomes important when two organisms strive for something that is not in adequate supply for both of them. Thus, plants compete for light and nutrients in a forest, and animals compete for food and shelter when the latter are relatively scarce in terms of the density of animals. If the population consists of only a few scattered individuals, competition will not be a factor of ecological importance. In the arctic, for example, plants may be so few and scattered due to the severe climate that no competition for light occurs.

The result of competition is that both parties (that is, the competition) are hampered in some manner. At the population level this means that density or rate of population energy flow, will be reduced or held in check by the competitive action. There is another type occurs when two organisms interfere with one another while striving for something even though that something is not in short supply. For example, the organisms might secrete substances that interfere with each other, or they might even eat each other. Many ecologists prefer not to include such direct mutual inhibition under the heading of competition.

Both intraspecific and interspecfic competition can be very important in determining the kinds and numbers of organisms. Intra-specific competition is an important factor in those populations that tend to be selfregulated in the manner described above. An interesting behaviour pattern, which results in intraspecific competition for space and a rather effective control of population size, is known as territoriality; it is characteristic of many species of birds and some other higher animals. At the beginning of the breeding season the male of a territorial species of bird will "stake out" a definite area of its habitat (that is, the "territory") and defend it against other males of the same species, with the result that no other ale is allowed to enter the area. Much of the loud bird song we hear in the spring is for the purpose of announcing to other males "ownership" of land, and not for the purpose of wooing the female, as is often supposed. A male that is successful in holding his land has a high probability of mating and nesting, while a male that is unable to establish such a territory will not breed. Once the pair is formed, the female also joins in the defense of the territory in many species. The defended territory also serves a positive purpose of insuring the complex business of caring for the nest and young will not be interrupted by the presence of other males and females. Finally, it should be mentioned that the actual defense of the territory does not usually involve much actual fighting or other severe stress. Would be invaders respect the established bird; loud songs or threat displays usually are sufficient to cause the invader to withdraw. However, if one of the pair should be killed it is very often quickly replaced by a bird form a reservoir of individuals not established. Therefore, since the territorial behaviour pattern helps avoid both overcrowding and undercrowding it can be siad to be regulatory in the sense that such behaviour promotes a sigmoid growth pattern, or at least helps prevent an overshoot of carrying capacity.

Plant populations, as well as animal populations, may regulate themselves, so to speak, and avoid overcrowding. As one drives through the desert in the southwestern United States one is impressed with the fact that desert shrubs are widely spaced, often almost uniformly distributed as if planted at regularly spaced intervals. The pattern would seem to be explained by competition for scarce water, which eliminates all but one individual in a given area. However, evolution of self-regulation of the population has occurred in some species, in that severe competition for water is avoided by the production of leaf or root hormones that inhibit development of other individuals in the neighborhood. That is, chemical substances rleased by decaying leaves that fall to the ground under the shrub, or by the living root in the soil, inhibit or kill any seedlings that may start to sprout. Such a control mechanism would tend to keep plants spaced apart, thereby reducing actual competition for water, which might result in stunting or death of all plants should there be many trying to grow in the same place. In this kind of "birth control" the quality of the individual in a limited environment is maximized, not the quantity; is there as lesson here for man?

Amensalism and antibiosis

Amensalism is an interspecific relationship in which one population is inhibited while the other is unaffected. A simple example is the shading out of certain plants under tall trees. The trees reduce the available sunshine at the ground level, and numerous species of plants cannot find adequate light in the shade. Hence, only shade-tolerant plants with lower light requirements can survive as ground cover in the forest.

Antibiosis is a specific type of amensalism in

which one organism produces a metabolite that is toxic to other organisms. The best known example is the mold, Penicillium, which produces an antibiotic substances causing the death of many bacteria. This was observed and identified in the classic work of Florey and Fleming in England in the late 1920's and early 1980's which led to the development of antibiotics in clinical medicine. Penicillin, strepotomycin, aureomycin and other antibiotics used against disease organisms all represent a similar ecologic principle, and one which is widespread in nature. Many species of fungi and lichens produce metabolic substances which inhibit bacterial growth. The green algae Chlorella produces substances which inhibit the growth of diatoms of the genus Nitzschia, and conversely, Nitzschia produces a substance which inhibits Chlorella.

Many plants also produce substances which are toxic or inhibitory to animals. Old cells of Chlorella produce a substance which inhibits the feeding of Daphnia. Algal blooms of some blue-green and red algae produce chemicals toxic to fish. The well known Red tide of southern coastal waters, produced by the flagellate Gymnodinium brevis, can result in massive fish kills.

Land plants also produce inhibitory substances. The roots of some species of trees produce substances which inhibits the growth of other trees, both of their own species and different species. This may result in a characteristic spacing pattern of trees within a forest, dependent not so much upon competition for sunlight at the conopy level, but upon competition for space, water or nutrients at the subterranean root level. Many plants produce substances toxic to animals which touch them or eat them. In Nevada and Utah the desert bush Halogeton glameratus produces oxalic acid which is poisonous to sheep. Poisonous toadstools to and tubers have been well known throughout the history of man. In South America and Africa, many native people harvest the tubers of the poisonous manioc plant, but they place it in a series of soaking vats to leach out the toxic chemicals before consuming the starchy tissue of the roots. A small African monkey, the talapoin monkey (Cercopithecus talapoin), has learned to steal the manioc from the soaking vats at just the proper state.

Many of these substances are in a class of compounds known as ectorines of environmental harmones. Ectorines are substances produced by the organism which affect other organisms of the same or different species. Not all ectocrines are toxic or inhibitory, of course; many are stimulatory or beneficial. But collectively, they represent chemical messengers by which individuals and species are interrelated.

Aggregations

All organisms react on their habitat in one way or another, and when they occur in numbers these reactions produce a conspicuous effect. Water conditioning occurs hence physical or chemical changes occur as the result of organisms living in it. Compared with unconditioned water, these changes may have either a harmful or a beneficial effect on organisms introduced into the water after the original organisms have been removed. Water is said to be homotypically conditioned when the changes were previously produced by individuals of the same species as being studied and heterotypically conditioned when the changes were produced by a different species.

Experimental studies have demonstrated that gold-fish grow faster in water that has been homotypicaly conditioned for 24 hours than in unconditioned water. Both fish and amphibian larvae also do better in water conditioned by the presence of mollusknes than in unconditioned water. The marine flatworm Procerodes wheatland will survive much longer when transferred to fresh water conditioned by the presence of either live or dead individuals of the same species or by freshwater species of flatworms than they do in unconditioned fresh water. The longer survival in toxic solutions, faster growth, and greater reproduction of protozoans, snails, flatworms, cladcerans, amphibian larvae, and fish occurring in aggregations rather than as isolated individuals is attributable to water conditioning.

Benefits derived from aggregating are shown in other ways by terrestrial animals. In honeybees, when hive temperatures drop below 14°C (57°F) during the winter, they form clusters and maintain a mass temperature several degrees above outside temperatures. This is brought about by increased metabolic oxidation of honey in their bodies and by increased muscular activity. Furthermore, the compact cluster presents a surface area for heat loss that is less than the total surface area of the individuals separately. When there is danger of overheating, the bees in the hive spread out on the combs and fan with their wings to create a circulation of air. They will also carry water into the hive and place small quantities both outside and inside the comb cells. The forced air circulation evaporates the water and cools the hive. Bees also cool themselves by constantly moving their tongues in and out of their mouths, exposing to evaporation the moisture that is present on them as a thin film temperature regulation is less well developed in other social Hymenoptera.

Allelochemistry

Included here are the coactions whereby chemicals secreted by one organism affects the growth, health, or behaviour of other organisms. Allelopathy is produced in plants when toxins are liberated that inhibit seedling growth in the vicinity. This may affect succession of plant species, especially important in the early stages. Some pioneer species in the abandoned field sere produce substances inhibitory to nitorgen-fixing and nitrifying bacteria. This retards invasion of other species that require higher nitrogen concentration in the soil. Volatile inhibitors are generally more prevalent than water-soluble ones, and relatively more prevalent in arid than humid climates. Antibiotics produced by bacteria, fungi, actinomycetes, and lichens are widespread in nature and may be one of the reasons why bacteria pathogenic to man cannot mutiply well in soils. A number of antibiotics, such as penicillin, have been used extensively in human medicine.

The use of allelochemic coactions agriculture has possibilities but has yet to be exploited.

Among animals, overcrowding of tadpoles in culture dishes in associated with the occurrence of peculiar round vacuolated cells in the intestinal tract and feces that appear responsible for curtailment of further growth (Rose 1960). Under laboratory conditions, killer stocks of Paramecium aurelia produce a toxin, paramecin, at the rate of one unit-particle per animals per 5 hours. One unit-particle is enough to kill one individual of sensitive stock of the same species as well as being lethal to other species of Paramecium. Conditioning that becomes unfavourable \homotypically may sometimes be favorable, or at least tolerable, heterotypically. Thus in protozoan infusions there is a microsere of one species succeeding another.

Allechemic effects are of great variety in both plants and animals: repellants, escape substances, suppressants, venoms, inductants, attractants, signals, stimulants, autotoxins, antoinhibitors, and so on. Pheromones chemical messages between members of a species especially important in reproductive behaviour, social regulation and recognition, alarm and defense, territory and trail marking, food location, as so on Many of these effects are beneficial to the individual; others serve for competitive purposes.

Protocooperation

In the positive relationship between populations, proto-cooperations is a short step ahead commensalism, to cooperation, both populations gain by the association or interaction of some kind. A considerable work on protocooperation was one by Alee (1938, 1951). In nature, crabs and coelenterates (sea anemone) are often found associated with each other. This association is of mutual benefit to both. The coelenterates grow on the back of the crabs, or sometimes planted there by the crabs. The coelenterates provide protection to the crabs. In turn, these are transported by crabs to new situations, which ensure them good supply of food. There is no physiological relationship betweeen the coelenterate and the crab, and none is absolutely dependent upon the other.

Conclusion

There exists complex relationships between different populations. Some of these relashionships play a vital role in the regulation of populations. Successful parasitism represents something of compromise between two populations. Predator-prey system is the product of long evolutionary process. A close relationship exists prey, but it is not always the case. The inter-specific competition is a basis to the theory of natural selection and evolution of species. While commensalism, proto co-operation and mutualism beautifully illustrate how interspecific relations can be beneficial.

Table showing interactions among species

Type of Interaction	*Species A*	*B*	*General nature of Interaction*
1. Neutralism	0	0	Neither population effects the other
2. Competition	-	-	Direct inhibition of one species by the other, or indirect inhibition when common resource is in short supply.
3. Parasitism	+	-	Population A, the parasite, generally smaller than B, the host.
4. Predation	+	-	Population A, the predator, generally larger than B, the prey.
5. Amensalism or Antibiosis	-	0	Population A inhibited, B not affected
6. Commensalism	+	0	Population A, the commensal, benefits while B, the host not affected.
7. Protocooperation	+	-	Interaction favorable or both but not obligatory.
8. Mutualism	+	+	Interaction favourable to both but obligatory.

0 Indicates no signification interaction.
+ Indicates beneficial effect on growth, survival or other population attributes
- Indicates harmful effect on growth, survival or other population attributes.

Type 2 and 5 can be classified as negative interaction, 6,7,8 as positive interactions, and 3,4 as both.

5 Population and Health

Health

The concept of Health has defied definition for decades. According to a working definition, "Health is physical, social and mental well-being with an added spiritual element". The most acceptable definition of health has been provided by the World Health Organisation and it defines health as a state of complete physical, mental and social well-being and not merely an absence of disease or infirmity. This definition underlines three major areas worth examining further i.e. physical, mental and social. It also points to an important aspects that simply freedom from disease does not constitute health.

Physical health

Physical health is a reflection of the optimal functions and appearances of the individual such as;

1. sound sleep;
2. regular activity of bowels and bladder;

3. smooth and co-ordinated movements;
4. intact senses and active reflexes; and
5. proper growth and development

Mental health

With the reiteration of the ancient concept of 'a sound mind in a sound body', it is now re-established that physical and mental health are related. Though it is rather difficult to define mental health, freedom from internal conflict, adjustment to adversities and self-control, are the signs of sound mental health. However, on account of its multi-dimensional nature, it is difficult to identify precise measures of mental health.

Social health

Social health can be measured on the basis of crime rate, illiteracy level, divorce rate and suicide rate.

Determinants of health

Health has been defined as a relative concept, where the spectrum-ranging from positive health to death-is so wide and fluctuating that it is difficult to ever maintain a status quo. The factors which determine the swing principally fall into five areas.

1. Human biology including genetic constitution;
2. Environment;
3. Ways of living;
4. Socio-economic status; and

5. Comprehensive health services.

Indicators of health

To be able to determine how healthy an individual or a community is, one first has to decide how to;

1. measure health;
2. compare health;
3. allocate resources;
4. apply policies and programmes; and
5. evaluate the services.

One needs a set of indicators which can measure health. Till today, health is viewed as a 'positive' concept; yet most of the indicators by which health is measured are 'negative' ones, such as ill health or poor health. Health can, therefore, be measured in terms of lack of health, through a set of variables, often referred to as indicators. However, these indicators have to be (a) sensitive; (b) specific; and (c) objective. The commonly used health indicators are listed and discussed below.

1. Mortality Indicators

(a) Crude death rate;

(b) Expectation of life at birth/one year of age;

(c) Infant mortality rate;

(d) Child mortality rate;

(e) Maternal mortality;

(f) Disease specific mortality; and

(g) Proportional mortality rate;

The mortality indicators only measure final outcomes and do not reflect on the quantum of sickness load in a society.

2. Morbidity indicators

(a) Incidence rate; and

(b) Prevalence rate of different diseases or disabilities.

The incidence rate takes into its numerator only the new cases of a disease in a specified period and the denominator is the population which is at risk or is exposed. This is generally used for evaluating effectiveness of control measures and also estimating the risk of developing a disease in the community.

The prevalence rate has as its numerator the number of existing cases of a disease over a specified period or at a point in time and the denominator is the total population. The prevalence rate is helpful in planning and administration and for measuring the magnitude and patterns of diseases and health needs.

3. Nutritional service indicators

Nutritions is the prime indicator of health, especially in the first few formative years of life. Nutritional status is used as one of the principal indicators of positive health and is assessed on the basis of a group of measures such as;

(a) Birth weight;

(b) Weight for age;

(c) Height for age;

(d) Weight for height;

(e) Mid-arm circumference; and

(f) Skin fold thickness.

4. Health care delivery indicators

(a) Doctor : Population ratio;

(b) Doctor : Nurse ratio;

(c) Bed : Population ratio;

(d) Population per health institution; and

(e) Population per traditional birth attendant.

5. Utilization rates

Health services, with all its vertical and horizontal expansion, should be easily available, culturally acceptable and economically affordable to enable attainment of the goal of health for all by A.D. 2000. The extent to which this is so, decides the utilization rates of these services by the community. The utilization rates of different services given an indicator of the need and demand, and in turn the health status. The rates are;

(a) Percentage of children under 2 years immunized against diphtheria, tetanus, pertusis, poliomyelitis, tuberculosis and measles;

(b) Percentage of women using antenatal services;

(c) Percentage of deliveries conducted by trained birth attendants;

(d) Bed occunancy rates; and

(e) Average duration of stay in hospital.

6. Social and mental health indicators

(a) Suicide rates;

(b) Crime rates; and

(c) Road traffic accident rates.

7. Socio-economic indicators

(a) Population increase rate;

(b) Per capita GNP;

(c) Levels of unemployment;

(d) Dependency ratio; and

(e) Adult literacy rate;

8. Indicators of quality of life

The Physical Quality of Life Index is a resultant sum of infant mortality, life expectancy at the age of one year and literacy.

Health in India

Health is a social goal and considered an integral component of the development process in the overall planning in India since independence. The importance of health in overall socio-economic development was well recognized and it was an important part of the Community Development Programme, started in 1952.

The State shall, in particular, direct its policy towards securing.... that the health and strength of workers, men and women, and the tender age of children are not abused and the citizens are not forced by economic necessity to enter avocations unsuited to their age or strength.

The State shall make provision for securing just and humane conditions of work and for maternity relief.

The State shall regard the raising of the level of nutrition and standard of living of its people and the improvement of public health as among its primary duties and, in particular, the State shall endeavour to bring about prohibition of the consumptions except for medicinal purposes of intoxicating drinks and drugs which are injurious to health.

For the realization of social objectives enshrined in our Constitution, the government initiated five year plans in which healths was identified as an important sector. With the sustained efforts in the last 42 years, significant improvement has been registered in the health status of the people. The most dreaded scourge, the smallpox has been totally eradicated; plague is no longer a problem as no human case has occurred for more than 20 years, malaria has been effectively brought under control thus saving millions of lives and its incidence is well below 2 million compared to 75 million prior to 1950; and deaths due to cholera have been significantly reduced. In a broader context of the changing scenario, the mortality rate too, has been reduced to less than half; the infant mortality from 135 to 96 per thousand live births; and life expectancy has gone up to 56 years from a mere 32 years.

These are no meagre achievements, yet they do not provide any room for complacency. The health situation in India is still a cause for serious concern. The population growth rate continues to be alarmingly high; maternal mortality and child mortality are distressingly high; the per capita calorie consumption is yet to match the recommended allowances, thus resulting in severe malnutrition, particularly among young children and expectant women, blindness, tuberculosis and leprosy continue to have incidence. Safe drinking water, which is necessary for controlling the water-borne diseases which account for half of the deaths from communicable diseases, is accessible to only one-third of the rural population and only 0.5 per cent enjoy basic sanitation amenities.

Health profile of India

India, despite significant changes and improvement in the health situation, still continues to struggle with numerous health problems. Communicable diseases continue to be a major cause of ill-health. The incidence of non-communicable disease is rising. Malnutrition is widely prevalent and the population explosion has further worsened the situation. On the one hand there is great scarcity of resources and on the other, there is uneven distribution of health care facilities.

The majority of health problems are the products of illiteracy, poverty, ignorance, overcrowding, poor environmental conditions and uneven distributions of health manpower and institutions.

Population explosion

With only 2.4 per cent of the global land area. India supports around 800 million people, i.e. about 15 per cent of the world's populations; and is the second most populous country in the world. At independence in 1947 we had 342 million mouths to feed and from then onwards the population has been growing at an alarming pace with a young population amounting to 40 per cent, thus increasing the dependancy ratio.

With the current growth rate, it is expected to reach the I billion mark by the turn of the century. The present situation is a result of uncontrolled fertility and consequent high birth-rate, coupled with a sharply declining death rate. A look at the population trend from 1901 reveals that except for a minor decrease in 11911-21, the year of the big divide, the growth rate has increased from 11 per cent in 1931 to 25 per cent in 1981, with an annual increase by 14 million. India is in the helpless situation where even if each couple today were to stop at two children, the population would still continue to increase.

Birth rate, Death rate and Natural growth rate in India, 1901-86

Year	*Crude Birth rate*	*Crude Death rate*	*Natural growth rate*
1901-11	49.2	42.6	6.6
1911-21	48.1	47.2	0.9
1921-31	46.4	36.3	10.1
1931-41	45.2	31.2	14.0

1941-51	39.9	27.4	12.5
1951-61	41.7	22.8	18.9
1961-71	41.2	9.0	22.2
1971-81	37.2	15.0	22.2
1971	36.9	14.9	22.0
1976	34.4	15.0	19.4
1981	33.9	12.5	21.4

Birth, Death & Natural growth Rate in India, 1981-86

The mounting population pressure has severely eroded the achievements of our planned development. The economy is severely battered. The per capital availability of food grains has decreased, despite food grain production having trebled in last 30 years. The exploding population, already extirpating available resources, needs additional resources too. It has been estimated that for a single year's increase in population, we need.

11,850,000	quintals of food grain;
180,000,000	meters of cloth;
2,391,000	hourses;
121,000	schools;
355,000	teachers; and
3,813,000	jobs.

The country's economy simply can not bear this additional burden, all the more when 50 per cent of the population is below the poverty line.

Not only this, the explosive situation has adversely affected maternal morality and infant mortality. The per capita expenditure on health has also gone down in the real sense, since 3 per cent of the total budget, which has remained stationary over successive five year plans, is now shared by a larger number of people and is also of less value with high inflation.

Mortality and morbidity

The death rate 11 to 12 per thousands population, still continues to be unacceptably high, though it has declined to less than half in the last three decades. Within the country itself, there are wide variations, ranging from 72 per thousand in Kerala, to 19.2 per thousand in Uttar Predesh. The major brunt of mortality is borne by the northern states, namely, Bihar, Madhya predesh, Orissa, Rajasthan and Uttar Predesh. The examination of major causes of deaths reveals that most of the deaths are due top communicable diseases, such as respiratory illness, gastro-intestinal disorder and fever. The recent trends also show a rise in-deaths due to non-communicable disease, such as cancers, cardiovascular diseases, metabolic disorders and accidents.

Infant and maternal mortality

The most affected groups in the population are children and women of child-bearing age. The infant mortality rate, though steadily declining, yet remains quite high. Of 1000 children born in India, about 100 die during the first year, 40 more die during the second year, 25 in the third year and 10 to 15 in the fourth and the fifth years. In other words, almost one-fifth of the number of children born die before they are five years old. Almost 1.5 million die of diarrhoeal disease, 1.5

to 2 million die of acute respiratory infections and about 1.3 million die of diseases preventable by immunization, mainly neo-natal tetanus and measles. Malnutrition is a major underlying cause of death, mortality doubling for each lower category of nutritional status.

The rate of decline in infant mortality is attributed to improvement in socio economic conditions control of communicable diseases, better nutrition, obstetric care, immunization against vaccine-preventable diseases, and better health awareness among people. The majority of infant deaths are attributed to factors that are manageable or preventable in nature.

Besides these direct causes, there are factors, cultural, social and economic, which contribute to high infant deaths. Those are; lower age of mother, order of birth, less interval between two births, large family size, high fertility, unheallty child rearing practices, low family income, non-availability of ante-natal and natal services, delivery by untrained dais and poor environmental conditions.

Most of these causes could be eliminated by improving the delivery of the comprehensive health-care package of MCH services, with emphasis on timely screening of high risk groups and a strong referral back up.

The other most vulnerable group consists of women of child-bearing age. India belongs to the category of countries, in which maternal mortality, ranging between 5 to 10 per thousand live-births, is the highest in the world. Maternal mortality accounts for more than 1 per cent of total deaths in the country and about 25 to 40 per cent of deaths among women. The major causes of high maternal mortality are disorders during pregnancy, i.e. haemorrhages, toxaemia and puerperal sepsis. Anaemia during preganancy has a compounding effect which is directly responsible for 20 per cent of maternal deaths and is associated indirectly with another 20 per cent of deaths among child-bearing mothers. The distribution of causes of maternal mortality are given in table 7.5 and figure 7.6

Maternal Mortality in India, 1976-80

Specific causes	1976	1977	1978	1979	1980
Abortion	11.6	8.2	11.0	11.7	12.5
Toxaemia	10.4	11.2	21.2	16.1	12.4
Anaemia	22.1	15.9	14.6	15.0	15.8
PPH	17.2	20.6	18.2	20.0	15.8
Malposition of foetus	8.4	9.4	9.5	10.5	3.4
Puerperal	13.5	18.8	12.4	11.7	12.4

Communicable diseases

Communicable diseases, as mentioned earlier, constitute a major threat to the health of the people in India. Some of them have been mentioned below.

Malaria: At one time, Malaria accounted for 8 lakh annual deaths with 75 million cases every year. This had a devastating effect on the nation's economy and health of the people. This disease was cut to size by 1961, the year which witnessed only 50,000 cases. Thereafter, malaria raised its ugly head again and in 1976 it affected 6.4 million people in the country. With effective control measures it is, however, declining; yet 1.6 million people suffered from malaria in 1987.

Tuberculosis: One of the important public health problems is tuberculosis. It has been estimated that 2 per cent of the total population above 10 years of age have the tubercular disease. There are about 10 million cases of tuberculosis and approximately 500,000 people die of it every year. However, there are indications of its declining trends.

Leprosy: Though not a fatal disease, leprosy is a leading cause of disability in India. According to estimates and reports available, about 4 million people suffer from leprosy, of which 20 to 25 per cent are infectious. Though the disease is endemic in the country, almost 50 per cent of leprosy cases are concentrated in the states of Andhra Predesh and Tamil Nadu.

Pohomyelitis: This is a major crippling disease, especially among young children in the country. About 200.000 children in the 0 to 5 years age-group become disabled due to poliomyelitis every year. On average, the prevalence rate is approximately 4 per 1000 pre-school children and the annual incidence varies between 1 to 3 per 1000 pre-school population.

Diphtheria, whooping cough, measles and tetanus; These diseases are endemic and their incidence is quite high particularly in childhood. They claim a heavy toll of lives in this vulnerable group and sizeably contribute to high infant and child mortality.

Cholera: Cholera is still a major threat to public health despite the fact that deaths due to cholera have been drastically reduced over the period of the last three decades. There were 86,997 reported deaths due to the cholera in 1950, which were reduce to only 2,642 in 1984. However, the disease is endemic and continues to pose a danger of assuming epidemic dimensions.

Diarrhoeal diseases: These claims a heavy to of lives in India, especially among children below 5 years of age. Over 1.5 million deaths are reported to be due to diarrhoeal diseases every years.

Trachoma: This still remains one of the major causes of blindness. In 5 per cent of the 9 million blind and 45 million visually handicapped, trachoma was the sole cause. The prevalence ranges from 0.5 per cent to 79 per cent in the country.

Sexually transmitted diseases. STDs, especially syphillis and gonorrhoea are almost endemic, and now AIDS joins them. With a very high mortality and virtually no available cure, it is naturally a point of concern. The mushrooming slums, illiteracy, migration, rapid urbanization and prostitution are some of the factors keeping up the endemicity levels.

Besides the above mentioned problems, several other diseases are commonly seen in the country, such as infective hepatitis, typhoid, worm infestations, filaria, guinea worm, kala-azar, meningitis, etc.

Non-communicable diseases

The success achieved in the control of communicable diseases contributed significantly to higher life expectancy and with that came up a number of non-communicable/metabolic diseases.

Cardiovascular disease: The heart bears the maximum brunt of development; the race to acquire material assets, and changing values, personal behaviour and habits, Hypertensions, coronary heart disease, Myocardial infarction, rheumatic heart disease and congenital heart defects, are all on the increase.

Incidence of cardiovascular disease in India

Type	*% of all cardiac diseases*
Rheumatic	30-40
Hypertension	20-25
Ischemic heart disease	11-15
Cor-pulmonale	10-20
Congenital heart disease	2-5

Diabetes: An estimate of a pilot survey conducted by the Diabetic Association of India indicates its high prevalence of 1 to 7 per cent. It is no more a disease of the elite and of executives. It is slowly but constantly on the rise, with genetic inheritance, acquired obesity and stress as the major causes and precipitating factors.

Cancer: Cancer is now one of the 10 leading causes of deaths in India with an incidence of one per 1000 population. It is a group of disease characterised by abnormal growth of cells. It invades tissues and eventually causes death.

Blindness and visual impairment: These diseases have put many people out of the normal stream of life. A sample survey by ICMR indicates a prevalence of 1.5 per cent. The principal causes are identifies as;

Cataract	55%
Trachoma	5%
Infections	15%
Malnutrition	5%
Injuries	1.25%
Glaucoma	0.5%

The National Sample Survey Organisation carried out a population-based survey and reported that 3,47 million were blind in 1981.

Health services-A hanging scenario

India inherited health care services from the British. In the pre-independence era, hardly any public health services existed, and whatever were available were mainly at the time of outbreaks of epidemics or communicable diseases. The services were mainly concentrated in the urban areas and were mostly curative in nature. The services were available to only the elite who could afford them. The facilities were practically inaccessible to the rural poor, the masses who needed them most. The Bhore Committee recommendations ushered in a new era in health care in India. It recommended health care on the basis of the concept of comprehensive health care, enunciating that health services.

1. should be preventive and promotive and not simply curative;
2. should be available to all, irrespective of ability to pay for them;
3. should be made available as close to the beneficiaries as possible;
4. should take care of vulnerable groups in the population, such as pregnant women and children; and
5. should encourage the participation of the community.

The health services started in 1952, were based on these very recommendations and through them significant changes could be achieved in the health situation of the country.

Health for all

The concept of health underwent revolutionary changes in 1977 when the Annual World Health assembly created history through a resolution that the main social target for countries should be 'attainment by all citizens of the world, a level of health that will permit them to lead a socially and economically productive life,' the goal being identified with health for all by the year A.D. 2000.

The 1978 conference at Alma Ata, officially reinforced the resolution and identified the primary Health Care approach as the key to attain the global goal of Health for all by 2000. This was followed by an endorsement from the world health assembly in 1979.

The central themes of the approach 'health for all through primary health care' are;

1. a universal coverage with essential health care that is relevant, effective, acceptable, accessible and affordable;
2. community participation in planning, providing and evaluating health care;
3. co-ordination between health and health-related sectors;
4. equitable distribution ensuring availability and accessibility of health services to all sections of the community, rich or poor, urban or rural; and
5. appropriate technology and optimal utilization of resources.

India, being one of the signatories to the Alma Ata declaration, has made a political commitment for attaining this goal to its people, and planners have come out with their concern about positive health and formulated a new health policy.

National health policy

The year 1983 proved to be the turning point in the history of health services in India, when an official draft of the health policy was placed before Parliament and was accepted for implementation. This reaffirmed the strong political will to attain

HFA and assured the masses of the best possible health policies and programmes to be implemented with their participation, promoting planned and co-ordinated socio-economic development. The political commitment is reflected in the policy and in the targets it set to be achieved in a phased manner.

National health programmes

Though health is a state subject, even before a national policy for health was adopted in order to combat major diseases and associated morbidity and mortality, various health programmes were undertaken at the national level. A few of them with their salient features are mentioned here.

1. National malaria eradication programme

Distinguished as the biggest health programme in any country against a single communicable disease, the NMEP launched in 1953, yielded spectacular results. Within five years, the number of cases of malaria was brought down from 75 million. Based on this success, the initial 'control' nature of the programme was converted to 'eradication'. The enthusiasm of eradication lasted only upto 1961 when an all time low of only 50,000 malaria cases were reported. Thereafter, the graph moved up again because of (a) increase in chloroquin resistance; (b) increase in insecticide resistance; (c) poor supply of insecticides; and(d) increase in cost of insecticides.

It reached a peak of 6.47 million cases in 1976. The situation called for shedding of the complacent attitude and indicated the need for a review. As a result, the 'control' nature of the NMEP was resorted with modifications and is now known as the 'Modified Plan of Action'. This strategy paid off, and the number of cases was brought down to 1.66 million in 1987, a reduction of the order of 74.3 per cent in 11 years.

2. National filaria control programme

The estimate is that about 360 million people are presently living in filaria endemic areas. The present strategy of the programme involves the repeated application of anti-larval and anti-parasite measures in urban areas and control through early detection and treatment of the cases in rural areas.

3. National tuberculosis control programme

The national Tuberculosis Control Programme was launched in 1963. It operates through District Tuberculosis Centres. There are about 371 such Centres and 335 TB Clinics. The programmes mainly undertakes (a) case finding; (b) treatment of cases; and (c) immunization with BCG vaccine. Under the NTCP all the required drugs are made available free of cost.

The management and treatment of TB has undergone revolutionary changes. Now the patient can take treatment at home which is as effective as hospitalization. Effective anti-tubercular drugs are made available; and short-term chemotherapy has been developed. These recent developments have greatly helped in the effective planning and control of tuberculosis.

4. National leprosy control programme

The programme was launched in 1955 to initiate the control against leprosy. It became a high priority programme after 1980, when leprosy control activities received a place in the 20-point programme and was renamed as 'Leprosy Eradication programme'.It aimed at disease-arrest in all the known cases of leprosy by the year A.D. 2000. The programme is operated through a network of 708 Leprosy Control Units, 943 Urban Leprosy Centres, 252 District Leprosy Units and 7400 SET Centres. The major activities under the programme are; (a) early detection of leprosy cases through surveys; (b) treatment with anti-leprosy drugs; (c) rehabilitation, both vocational and social; and (d) health and social education.

5. Diarrhoeal disease control programme

An action plan has been developed to prevent the deaths due to diarrhoeal disease, including the control of cholera. The major activity under the programme is the promotion of Oral Rehydration Therapy through a massive media campaign. The Oral Rehydration Salt is supplied free of cost down to village-level to prevent deaths due to dehydration resulting from diarrhoea. It has been found very effective, especially with children, and is reported to have averted a larger number of deaths in this vulnerable group.

6. National guinea worm eradication programme

Guinea worm disease is endemic in a majority of states in India and amounts to a major public-health problem. The Eradication Programme was initiated in 1983-84. The programme undertakes; (a) an active search for cases twice a year at the village level; (b) periodical chemical treatment of water during peak seasons with Temephos; (c) personal prophylaxis; (d) health education; and (e) management of the cases.

7. National programme for prevention of blindness

This programme was launched in 1976 with the ultimate aim of reducing blindness in the country from 1.4 per cent to 0.3 per cent by the year A.D. 2000. The operational strategy includes health education, and providing comprehensive eye health care at the existing peripheral, intermediate and apex levels of health care. Two major activities are; conducting cataract operations through mobile eye camps and static units; and prevention of nutritional blindness through supplementation with Vitamin A.

8. Universal immunization programme

This programme is a major endeavour in improving the child survival rate in the country. Initiated as the 'Expanded Programme of Immunization' in 1978, it attacks six major diseases of childhood i.e. diphtheria, whooping cough, tetanus, tuberculosis, measles and poliomyelitis. In 1985, the programme changed its strategic approach and emphasis. It was renamed as the 'Universal Immunization Programme', focussing mainly on children below the age of 1 year and pregnant women. The programme aims to immunized he child with 3 doses of DPT and OPV, 1 dose of BCG and measles vaccines before the completion of one year of life and provide; two doses of tetanus toxoid to all pregnant women. Under the programme, immunization services have been strengthened with material, cold-chain equipment and effective logistics support. The programmes is yielding satisfactory results, providing coverage to an average of 50 per cent of eligible children and mothers. As a result of the UIP, there has been a significant reduction in deaths due to immunizable childhood diseases.

Besides these national health programmes, many other programmers are also in operation, namely;

1. National Family Welfare Programme;
2. National Water-Supply and Sanitation programme;
3. Integrated Child Development Services;
4. National Goitre Control Programme;
5. National Programme for Control of STDs and AIDS;
6. Programme for Prophylaxis against Anaemia; and
7. Minimum Needs programme.

6 Population and Nutrition

Nutrition is an important environmental factor which influences health and well-being. Nutritional status is determined by a number of considerations, and two of the important ones are food intake and infection. The relationship between nutrition and health is a two-way one. malnutrition can predispose an individual to ill-health and ill-health in turn adversely affect nutritional status. Malnutrition, unfortunately, is widespread in India and is a serious public health concern. It causes a great deal of suffering to many segments of the population, but particularly to women and children. Malnutrition is also responsible, both directly and indirectly, for the high rate of child death.

All the nutrients needed by man to maintain good health have to come through food-calories, proteins, vitamins, minerals and trace elements. The quantity and quality of the habitual diet therefore determine whether or not sufficient amounts and proper proportions of the nutrients are taken in. The reasons for insufficient intake of food by large sections of the population are several. Family incomes seems to be the single most important one, since purchasing power largely decides the amount and type of foods that can be afforded. This alone, however, does not explain all aspects of the issues.

Factors affecting food intake

Economic status and food intake

In earlier years, malnutrition at the national level was considered to be predominantly a 'food' problem of malnutrition could be checked. It is becoming increasingly clear that, while increases in food availability at the national level is a prerequisite for controlling malnutrition, this in itself is not enough, because what determines the habitual diet of a family is its purchasing power, even when the per capital availability increases. Food grain production in India increased almost three-fold, from around 50 million tonnes in 1951 to about 150 million tonnes in 1986, but the increase in population during the period, has to a considerable extent offset the agricultural gains. Despite the increments in the per capital availability, there being more food available per person, the problem of malnutritions has remained, because the real purchasing power of the lower income groups has not changed much.

As incomes rise, the amount and quality of the food eaten, progressively improve-the better quality being reflected in more diverse foods being consumed and in the inclusion of greater amounts of the so-called protective-food such as milk, fruits and vegetables. As may be expected, beyond a critical level of income, further improvements do not occur. Low-income families spend a much higher proportion of family income on food than the well-to-do. Sometimes this reaches as high a percentage as 80 to 85 per cent.

When purchasing power is so low that it is not enough to meet the food needs of the family, at constant income the family size will determine the amount of food eaten by each member in that family. There is an inverse relationship between calorie intake and family size, in both urban and rural families. Daily intake is below 2000 calories per person when the family size is between five and six, and more than 2000 calories when the family size is smaller-between four and five. This factor is often sufficient to make a difference in nutritional status.

Food beliefs and food taboos: Effects on food intake

important as income is, it is not the only determinant of food intake. Even when incomes permit, there are situations which can limit food and nutrient consumption. Food beliefs and food taboos strongly influence the choice of foods and restrict the use of some food articles, thus compromising nutritional status, particularly of children and women. Many of the food taboos and beliefs are independent of socio-economic status or educational level,but the consequences of practicing these beliefs are left mostly among the poor, because of the restricted variety which they can afford.

The concept of 'hot' and 'cold' foods is an example. Because of this belief, some foods are not consumed during certain seasons. Also, avoiding certain foods during pregnancy is widely practiced, in the belief that they are harmful to the foetus. Lactating women also avoid some foods in the belief that they are harmful to the baby, since they come into their breast milk. Other foods are included in the belief that they increase milk secretion. Scientific studies which have examined the truth of these beliefs have, by and large, not supported these claims.

Food considered 'hot in one part of the country, or even by one community, are considered 'cold' in another part and vice versa, supporting the contention that many of these food beliefs are largely culturally determined and pass on from one generation to the next. This, however, is not to say that all beliefs are wrong or to deny that some individuals show subjective feelings attributable to what are considered 'hot' or 'cold' foods.

Feeding practices during infancy: Effect on food intake

A lack of knowledge on the part of the mothers about the actual food needs of infants and children is another reason for insufficient food intake, even though there may be sufficient purchasing power. The concept that growing children need relatively more food than adults do is fairly widespread, but its quantitative aspect is not sufficiently appreciated by many mothers. They are often surprised to learn that the amount of food which a two or three-years old child needs, is almost one-half of what an adult man needs. They are also often not aware that because of the bulk, a young child has to be fed small amounts frequently-sometimes in as many as five or six eating sessions-if its needs are to be met. Many children remain underfed as a result of failure to appreciate these two facets of child nutrition.

Two other feeding practices based upon misconceptions contribute to under-feeding during infancy and lead to serious nutritional consequences during the first year of life. The first is the widespread practice, particularly seen in rural families, to exclusively breast-feed infants upto a year or more. Almost 50 per cent of mothers do so. They delay weaning i.e. the introduction additional food. The second is the practice of giving only token amounts, even when weaning foods are introduced. Many mothers wrongly believe that as long as the child is bread fed, it does not need other foods-a misconception which is the basis of practicing prolonged exclusive breast-feeding. Lack of knowledge about the nutrient needs is the basis of the second practice., For a great majority of infants, breast milk alone is enough to supply nutrient requirements only upto six months of age, no matter how well the mother is lactating. Additional foods must be introduced at the latest by the age of six months. If this is not done, the child's growth will suffer and this retardation cannot be corrected later on.

Feeding practice during sickness: Effects on food intake

A practice which limits food intake, which again is independent of income, is related to feeding during illness. It is customary to change the type of food and the amount during an episode of sickness. This is an almost universal practice and the change can be best described as putting the person on a 'semi-starvation' diet. The usual solid food is quickly replaced by either a semi-solid or wholly liquid diet in restricted quantities, till the sickness is over and sometimes even well past the illness. The restriction is often severe, amounting to over 50 per cent. This is done not merely in cases of gastrointestinal infections in which abdominal pain, vomiting and diarrhoea are present, but in every type of infection including simple fevers, coughs and colds. This practice is independent of the economic and educational status of the family, and is frequently suggested and supported wrongly by medical advice. The consequences of this altered feeding schedule are very different depending upon whether the family is a poor one or a well-to-do one. In the better-off households the child is usually well nourished when it develops the infection; prompt medical care is provided which restricts the severity and duration of illness and therefore the duration of semi-starvation. After recovery, the child is encouraged to 'catch-up' by eating of particularly nutritious foods. In contrast, a child from a poor family is already malnourished when it develops an infection; medical care is either delayed or not available, which delays the control of infection and therefore prolongs semi-starvation. 'Catch-up' eating cannot be afforded. Such a child fails to recover the lost ground and does not get back to its original nutritional status. Also, a child from a poor household is predisposed to repeated attacks of infections, unlike one from a well-to-do family, and the repeated semi-starvation episodes progressively worsen the child's nutritional status. Thus, the altered feeding practice during sickness, has little nutritional implications in a well-to-do family but has serious repercussions in a poor one.

An infections by itself is detrimental to nutritional status and the superimposition of the culturally-determined feeding practices can be truly serious. Educating communities particularly women, in the proper feeding of children during sickness, emphasizing that regular diets should be continued through all infection, including gastrointestinal,becomes an important component of health education.

Food intake is thus determined by a variety of factors. They include purchasing power, knowledge regarding food needs of individuals , feeding practices during health and particularly during sickness, and food beliefs and food taboos. Since food make directly influences nutritional status, it is obvious that these very factors affect nutritional status as well.

Nutritionally vulnerable groups

Malnutritions affects all segments of the population; but the risk of developing malnutritions and its health consequences are more serious during some periods of life than at others. The growing foetus during the last three months of pregnancy, the infant and the child up to the age of five years-more particularly up to the age of three years-are at much higher risk than others. These are periods of very rapid growth and the effects of food deprivation during these periods are more serious than when growth has slowed down. Women, during pregnancy and lactation, are also at increased risk. A pregnant woman needs additional nutrients for two purposes; to support the rapidly growing foetus, and to meet her own increased demands for carrying pregnancy to term. The common saying that an expectant mother should ear for two is however not strictly true. The additional amount of food she needs is roughly one-fifth to one-sixth of what she takes in her non-pregnant conditions.

The nursing mother needs additional nutrients mainly because of the breast-milk which she secrets. Contrary to popular belief, the ability of a mother to successfully breast-feed her child is not impaired as a result of malnutritions, unless she is severely malnourished. Practically all rural women in India, even those with mild and moderate degrees of malnutrition, secrete enough milk for their infants to grow properly. They continue to secrete milk upto a year and sometimes even beyond two years, though the quantities become progressively less. The composition of the milk they produce is also satisfactory, except that the concentrations of some vitamins are low, reflecting her own low dietary intake of these vitamins. The additional nutrients which a lactating woman has to take, are primarily to see that her own nutritional status will not deteriorate as a result of her feeding the baby. The additional demands of lactation, during the first six months, are greater than the demands made by pregnancy. She needs to eat additional food amounting to a third or more of her intake before she became pregnant.

The pregnant woman, the nursing woman, the growing foetus, the infant and the pre-school age child are together known as the vulnerable groups from the nutrition standpoint.

Nutrition and fertility

Malnourished population are generally thought to have higher fertility rates than do well-nourished populations. This high fertility rate, it has been suggested, set up a vicious circle. Contrary to this belief, malnutrition, if anything, has the opposite effect-it limits fertility.

Sex ratio

The sex ratio in a population influences fertility rate. In all developed countries, the ratio is over 1000, while in most developing countries, it is below 1000. In india, there are only 935 females per 1000 males in the total population. There are age-related trends. From birth upto age 12, the ratio progressively falls, it shows a rise thereafter, and from the 25th years onwards, it falls again till the age of 50. The fall is particularly steep between 25 to 35 years of age-an observation which is in keeping with the finding that maternal mortality rate is particularly high after the third parity. At no age does the ratio reach 1000. This age trend is in marked contrast to that seen in developed countries, where right from birth the ratio is over 1000 and slowly rises with age, with an abrupt increase after the age of 50 years.

The decline in the sex ratio in India between 1 and 12 years is due to the higher mortality among female infants and pre-school children, while the fall in the ratio during the child-bearing age is due to the high maternal mortality. Malnutrition plays a considerable role in causing the high mortality rates during these two periods of life. The low sex ratio during the active reproductive period seems to be a characteristic feature of countries which have malnutrition as a public health problem and can limit fertility. What this implies is that if female mortality rates are brought down and the sex ratio rises, the fertility rates will also rise, if other factors remain unchanged.

Age at menarche

Manarche, the first menstrual period, signifies sexual maturity. Socio-economic status is an important factor which influences the age at menarche. In India, the mean age at which it occurs is higher by about one year, in girls of low socio-economic groups as compared to girls of the high socio-economic groups. Rural girls attain menarche a little over a year later than do urban girls. Nutrition is one of the factors causing these differences. With increasing degrees of malnutrition, age at menarche was found to progressively increase from 13.7 years in normal girls to 15.2 years in severely malnourished girls, within a rural community.

Body weight is an important criterion. On an average, indian girls attain menarche when they reach a body weight between 32 and 36 kg. Since malnutrition delays the attainment of this weight, it also delays the age at menarche. Even among normal girls, at any given age, those who have started menstruating are heavier and taller than those who have not.

This delay in the age at meanarche due to malnutrition, is unlikely to influence fertility rates to any significant extent. What is really relevant is the age at marriage and age at first pregnancy.

Pregnancy outcome

A woman's ability to conceiver is not affected by malnutrition, except when it is very severe. The proportion of women who fall into this category is very small. But, once conception has occurred, both the course and outcome of pregnancy are affected by nutritional status.

Among women in poor socio-economic groups whose diets are poor and who are malnourished, between 20 and 30 per cent of pregnancies end in abortions and miscarriages. Among the well nourished. High pregnancy wastage is thus an outcome of poor nutritional status, resulting in lower fertility rates. The reduction is less than what is apparent, because abortions merely delay the birth of the next child. Sometimes within weeks, and often within months following an abortion, women become pregnant again.

Lactation amenorrhoea

Practically all mothers, in malnourished communities breast-feed their babies for long periods of time, because of cultural and economic reasons. Many do so upto two years and some even beyond this age. Breast-feeding delays the resumption of menstruation because of hormonal changes and women who are successfully breast-feeding their children, are relatively infertile. Even when contraception is not practiced, breast-feeding postpones pregnancy. In our country, the mean time-interval between two pregnanceis among rural women who do not resort to any family planning method is a little over 30 months. Shortening the duration and frequency of breast-feeding results in quicker restoration of fertility. The mean duration of amenorrhoea in rural Indian women who practice prolonged breast-feeding is almost 18 months compared to only 10 months among the urban women who breast-feed only upto 18 months.

Fertility foods

The belief that certain types of diets or some specific foods alter fertility, has no scientific support. Malnutrition, however, acts as a constraint on fertility. The observation that poor families have more children than do richer families, is because contraception is more often practiced by the latter. This masks the real higher-fertility potential in this group. If the nutritional status of the poor is improved without simultaneously bringing in other socio-economic changes, the result would be a significant increase in birth rate. This emphasizes the need for an integration of nutrition improvement programmes with fertility control programmes and other development activities to ensure that improved nutritional status will not lead to population growth, which would otherwise occur. Also, acceptance of family planning methods may be expected to improve when a higher infant-and child-survival rate can be ensured through improved nutrition. Significant and sustained reduction in birth rates are always preceded by significant and sustained reduction in death rates.

Nutrition and child survival: Implications for family limitation

The child mortality index in India is over 12 per cent as compared to less than 0.2 per cent in developed countries. This means that 12 out of every 100 children born, do not live to see their fifth birthday. This has important repercussions on life expectancy, the age structure of the population, the child turnover rate and acceptance of the small family norm.

Birth weights

The birth weight of an infant depends on many factors, of which nutrition of the mother, both before and during pregnancy, is an important one. Mothers from malnourished communities deliver babies with a mean birth weight of 2.7 kg, which is 0.6 kg lower than the mean birth weight of babies delivered by mothers of well nourished groups. premature and still births are much more common among malnourished mothers. Also, twice as many babies born to mothers from malnourished populations have birth weight below 2.5 kg. These differences, attributable to socio-economic differentials, are world-wide phenomena and affect infant survival and growth.

The reasons for the low birth weight of babies born to undernourished mothers are two-fold. One is the insufficient food intake during pregnancy. This can be corrected to some extent by providing enough food even in the late stages of pregnancy-the last 6 to 9 weeks. The other is the low weight and height of the woman at the time of pregnancy. If a woman weighs less than 38 kg before pregnancy, less than 42 kg during the last month of pregnancy, and if she is less than 145 cm in height, the chances of her having a low-birth-weight baby are very high. Close to 20 per cent of Indian rural women and women in urban slums fall into these categories. The women are short and underweight because they are malnourished during their early childhood. Their short stature cannot be corrected.

Infant mortality rate

The infant mortality rate in our country is currently about 100, a figure which is lower than the 140 which was reported a few years ago. There is a rural-urban differences, it being always higher in the rural areas. Many of the infant deaths-close to 50 per cent occur during the first month of life. prematurity and low birth weight are the most important causes. They increase the risk of fetal infections. In addition, low-birth-weight babies do not grow as well, as do normal babies. Coupled with delayed weaning and insufficient feeding, many of them become malnourished, develop severe infections and die during the second half of infancy. Not all the blame for infant mortality can be attached to malnutrition. Other poverty-related causes, such as insufficient obstetric care, poor environmental sanitation, over-crowding, unsafe drinking water and lack of timely medical care also contribute to high infant mortality.

Child mortality rate

Malnutrition is also responsible for a number of deaths among older children. Two out of every 100 children in the 1 to 5 year-old group die. Some die because of severe frank deficiency diseases, while others die because of diseases supported by malnutrition-diarrhoea, bronchopneumonia, measles, tuberculosis and viral infections.

This high child mortality promotes the desire in rural communities to have more children than they actually want and creates a resistance towards the small family norm. Parents of children who die in infancy usually have another child within the year, sooner than they otherwise would have. This increases the birth rate; it also shortens the inter-pregnancy interval. This short interval, apart from placing the mother at risk of becoming malnourished, also leads to the delivery of a low birth-weight infant. The child turnover rate becomes high and this is one of the reasons for the country's high child population-a vulnerable group which needs special nutrition care.

Family size and nutritional status

As indicated earlier, family size may be expected to determine the amount of food available to each member of the family and therefore nutritional status, particularly when income is limited. There is in fact an inverse relationship between family size and nutrient intake. Among families with two adults and three children or less, the mean intake of calories and protein is higher than that of families consisting of two adults with four or more children. The children in calories intake is close to 300 and that in protein intake is about 10g per day. In close to 60 per cent of families these differences mean either sufficiency of nutrition. This is reflected in differences in nutritional status particularly of children and pregnant women.

Over 60 per cent of children who suffer from severe protein-energy malnutritions come from large families and their birth orders are 4 or above. Less than 40 per cent of the first three born have such severe malnutrition. The growth status of children in large families is also less satisfactory than those of children in small families. Children with birth orders of three or below are almost 4 cm taller and 1.5 kg heavier than are children whose birth orders are 4 or above. Clinical signs of deficiency diseases are also seen more frequently among children from large families. Mild protein-energy malnutrition and vitamin A deficiency are seen in twice as many children whose birth orders are land above as compared to the earlier born.

The number of pregnancies a woman has, influences her nutritional status. Of all the women who have deficiency signs, almost two-thirds are those who have had 4 pregnancies or more. Also, anaemia and signs of deficiency of B-complex vitamins occur twice as frequently in women who have been pregnant four times or more,as compared to those who have had fewer pregnancies.

On the basis of these observations, it has been suggested that if the number of children in a family is restricted to a maximum ofthree, almost 60 per cent of malnutrition among young children and pregnant women can be eliminated without any other effort. The nutritional benefits are likely to be even more because the food and child care now going to the later born, would be diverted to the first three children, further reducing the quantum of malnutrition. It has to be recognized that limiting the number of children cannot be done in isolation; but when it can be achieved, the nutritional benefits can be substantial.

Some common nutritional deficiency diseases and their health consequences

Malnutrition-primary and secondary causes

If a nutritional disorder develops because the intake of a nutrient through food is insufficient, it is described as having arisen from a primary deficiency. This can only be corrected by improving the dietary intake of the nutrient. Not infrequently nutritional diseases develop, even when dietary nutrient intakes are enough, because there are other reasons. Such cases are described as having arisen from secondary deficiencies. Important among the reasons for secondary deficiencies are infections, defects in absorption, increases in losses of nutrients and, occasionally, medicines taken to control other diseases. In such cases correction is best achieved by removing the secondary cause, although improving intakes will also helps. In practice, both are done.

Stages in the development of deficiency diseases

There is usually a time-lapse of several days or weeks after intake of nutrients are lowered and before the disease becomes evident. There are several stages in between. The first stage is when the body-stores of the nutrient are reduced. This is followed by changes in the tissues although there is still no visible change. Laboratory tests will, however, show that changes have set in. When this situation has persisted for some time, actual signs and symptoms, which this situation has persisted for some time, actual signs and symptoms, which are easily seen, make their appearence. If in a community or population group there are several people with clinical disease, it it presumptive evidence that there will be many more with biochemical deficiency and even more in the depletion stage. The nutritional status of that populations is, clearly, unsatisfactory. Corrective action needs to be initiated note merely for those who actually have the disease but for the community as a whole.

In our country large number of people suffer from advanced clinical stages of many nutrient deficiencies indicating that all is not well with our population groups. There are wide regional variation in the extent and nature of the nutrient deficiency disorders. Some however are common to most parts of the country and are of serious public health concern. Four such diseases are briefly described here; protein-energy malnutritions in children, vitamin A deficiency, anaemia, and goitre due to iodine deficiency. They all share some common features. They are widespread, they contribute to increased illness and death, and they affect the quality of life by interfering with physical, social and mental development. Also they are all completely preventible-the knowledge and the means of doing so are available.

Protein-energy malnutrition

It was earlier believed that this disease among children came from their eating foods which did not have enough protein. This belief is incorrect. The diets of children of even poor families have a protein concentration which is satisfactory in spite of being predominantly vegetables-food based. The reason for this disease is that these foods are not eaten in sufficient amounts and this food-gap leads to secondary protein deficiency because, in the absence of sufficient calories, some of the protein is used for the purpose of providing energy. This has very important implications in the treatment, control and prevention of the disease.

Anywhere between 3 and 5 per cent of children below the age of five years living in rural India and urban slums have the serious clinical forms of protein-energy malnutrition and, if not promptly treated, will die. Several hundred thousand children die of this condition every year in our country. This figure of 3 to 5 per cent is a high one, but it is only the tip of the iceberg-over 70 per cent of children in this age group suffer from mild and moderate forms of the disease. Unlike in he severe clinical forms, there is nothing dramatic to observe in these mild and moderate cases. They show growth retardation, which can easily be missed except by the trained eye. A four year-old malnourished child will be shorter and lighter than what he should be for his age, and will look like a normal three year old child. Unless the age is known, he will pass off as a younger normal child. With a child population of nearly 110 million in this age group and almost 75 per cent of them living either in rural areas or urban slums, this means that over 50 million children in the country are malnourished. The seriousness of this lies in the fact that many of these children will have varying degrees of social and mental underdevelopment which persists in their adult lives. They also grow up into small-sized adults, with low stamina, low physical-work-capacity and therefore low productivity. The small size sometimes restricts their earning capacity.

There are marked differences in the body size of adults, depending on their socio-economic status. The rural adult man has an average height of 160 cm and an average weight of 52 kg, both of which are much lower than those of adults who come from well-to-do sections of the population. The rural adult woman is just 152 cm tall and weighs a mere 42 kg. This short stature and low weight has special significance for women because they influence the birth weights of their infants; and-low birth weight, as indicated earlier, is related to infant mortality.

Diet survey data from many parts of India show that almost one-third of the children in poor families do not eat enough food needed for normal growth. On top of this, the poor environmental sanitation around them predisposes them to infection. Thus both primary and secondary causes act together to produce malnutrition. Some maternal characteristics add to the problem. Even among the poor families, not all children suffer from malnutrition, and this can be related to differences in maternal qualities. Though they all come from the same rural, poor socio-economic strata, they differ in their knowledge about food, nutrition and health problems, their resourcefulness, their concern for the welfare of their children, their interaction with their infants and children, as also their general intelligence as judged by psychological tests. Mothers whose children are malnourished have lower scores in all these areas as compared to mothers whose children have no malnutrition. Maternal attributes therefore play an important role.

Vitamin a deficiency

Of all the vitamins, deficiency of Vitamin a is the most serious in our country, though it is not the most common. In its mild form vitamin a deficiency interferes with the ability to see in dim light which can be totally corrected by giving the vitamin. It can also lead to the development of greyish-white patches on the conjunctives which also is curable. In its severe forms, vitamin A deficiency damages the eye, leading to blindness which cannot be corrected. Vitamin A deficiency signs are rare below the age of one year and it affects mostly children upto the age of live. Older school-going children are also at risk.

Between 2 and 4 per cent of children in rural areas and urban slums have signs of mild vitamin A deficiency. The exact figures for the severe forms are not known with certainty, but it is calculated that about 30,000 children go blind very year as a result of vitamin A deficiency. The disease has now acquired a new dimension following the finding in some developing countries that even mild vitamin A deficiency increases the risk of mortality in young children. The public health importance and social repercussions of vitamin A deficiency are obvious.

The major reason for this disease is the fact that the diets of poor rural households do not contain enough vitamin A. Vitamin A is present only in foods animal origin, which are beyond the reach of the poor. Vegetarians depend upon foods which contain B-carotene for their vitamin A requirement. This is contained in all fruits and vegetables which have a yellow or green colour, and is converted to vitamin A in the body. What is unfortunate is that these relatively inexpensive dietary sources of vitamin A are not included in the diets of young children because of either ignorance or food taboos and beliefs.

Anaemia

The magnitude of the problem of anaemia second only to that of protein-energy malnutrition. For a long time it was believed that anemia was mostly a disease of women during their reproductive age. It is now known that anaemia occurs in people of all ages of both sexes right from infancy. Over 70 per cent of young children, 65 per cent of adult women and 45 per cent of adult men in our country have varying degrees of anaemia. Pregnant women, are the worst sufferers: almost 75 per cent have the disease.

The problem is less severe in urban than in the rural areas. The most important cause of anaemia is deficiency of iron. Through the diets of even the poor-contain fairly good amounts of iron, deficiency develops since much of this iron cannot be absorbed because of the nature of the diet.

Anaemia reduces work capacity and

productivity, which is particularly important in the context of the agricultural economy of the country. If anaemia is severe, it affects the growth and development of infants. It also affects the intellectual functioning of children. Even when anaemia is mild, it shortens attention span and lowers the ability to concentrate. Anaemia subjects therefore perform poorly in mental tasks which depend heavily on these two inputs. Anaemia children tend to show poor scholastic achievements.

Moderate to severe anaemia during pregnancy leads to the delivery of infants with low birth weights in addition to contributing to maternal mortality.

These health consequences of anaemia make the disease a problem of serious concern.

Goitre and iodine deficiency disease

Goitre is caused by deficiency of iodine and results in a visible enlargement of the thyroid gland which is situated in the neck. Unlike the previous three diseases, it is not found uniformly all over the country. Iodine deficiency is most often primary, there being insufficient intake through water and food. Secondary deficiency also occurs due to the presence of substances in the diet known as goitrogens. These substances interfere with the utilization of iodine in the body.

According to recent estimates about 40 million Indians have goitre. They are mostly seen in the goitre-belt, which stretches across the entire sub-Himalayan area. This includes parts of Jammu and Kashmir, Himachal Pradesh, Punjab, Haryana, Bihar, Uttar Pradesh, Meghalaya, West Bengal, Tripura, Manipur, Nagaland and Arunachal Pradesh. New goitre zones have recently been identified in Maharashtra, Madhya Pradesh and Karnataka.

Apart from causing visible and ugly enlargement of the thyroid gland, iodine deficiency has serious health implications for infants, children and pregnant women. About 15 per cent of school children in some goitrous areas have varying degrees of mental underdevelopment. About the same proportion of infants have biochemical abnormalities indicative of potential underdevelopment. Severe iodine deficiency during pregnancy results in the birth of incurable deaf-mute infants.

Besides these four major nutritional diseases, large sections of the population suffer from deficiencies of the vitamin B-complex group. Though widespread, this deficiency does not have the same degree of serious health-consequences. Deficiencies of vitamins C and D do occur but are not of a magnitude to be considered public health problems.

Gender difference in food intake and nutritional status

It is widely believed that in many households, particularly when the family is poor, boys and men enjoy preferential treatment over girls and women in the matter of food. The higher mortality and morbidity seen among girls and the higher incidence of the severe forms of malnutrition among girls have been ascribed to this discrimination in food intake. The overall sex ratio in the country is against the female. There are only 935 females for every 1000 males except in the state of Kerala where it is 1035. This has also, in part, been attributed to nutrition, because it is again widely believed that the nutritional status of women is less satisfactory than that of men leading to higher mortality among women.

These beliefs are based more upon impressions than on reliable scientific findings. While it is true that death rates among females throughout childhood and the reproductive age of 15 to 45 years are higher than in males, national diet survey and nutrition survey data, by and large, do not show that the dietary intakes and nutritional status of girls are less satisfactory than those of boys. These findings do not support the popular view that in the matter of food distribution within the family, even among the poor, parents discriminate against the female. That there is perhaps no discrimination in food allotment, it confirmed by the finding that the profiles of growth of boys and girls are similar. Among adult men and women too it is seen that neither with respect to food intake nor with respect to nutritional status are women worse off than men in rural communities. These findings do not imply that the matter is settled because in some areas and in some communities there is evidence that discrimination food, intake exists and that the nutritional status of women is worse than that of men. In view of the serious sociological and national implications, it is necessary to examine this question in depth.

The higher mortality rates in women and the higher incidence of severe malnutrition among girls have to be explained as being related to factors other than food and nutrition. It has been repeatedly seen that there is obvious discrimination in the matter of health care. During sickness more boys are taken to the hospital more promptly for 'good' medical care than girls. More girls are taken to less qualified village 'doctors'. Among children who need medical attention but do not get it, girls constitute a higher proportion. Discrimination against girls usually increases as their number in the household increases. This may explain why,even when there is no significant discrimination in the matter of food, more girls than boys develop the fatal, serious forms of malnutrition. There seems to be an even greater discrimination with respect to schooling, literacy and vocational training-all of which in later life contribute to shortcomings in maternal attributes which influences child rearing, including good nutritional status. In recent years it appears that the extent of discrimination is decreasing.

National nutrition programmes

Realizing the importance of nutrition in health and national development, the central and state governments have initiated several country-wide programmes to improve the nutritional staus of the population. Some of these are direct nutrition interventions aimed at eradicating the major, widespread specific deficiency diseases. Others are indirect nutrition programmes which help to improve overall food consumption, both in terms of quantity and quality.

Agriculture-related programmes which promote food production, and schemes which provide subsidized foods to the poorer sections come under the indirect category. Anti-poverty schemes such as the food-for-work programme., employment guarantee schemes, other income-generating plans and developmental activities also fall into this category. So do efforts aimed at nutrition and health education. The recently launched Universal Immunisation programmes which envisages the protection of all children against diphtheria, tetanus, whooping cough, tuberculosis, measles and poliomyelitis, should also be looked upon as an indirect nutrition programme because by reducing these infectious diseases, it can promote better nutrition. The importance of this, however, should not be overestimated, because these immunizations do not take care of the most common and important infection-respiratory, gastro-intestinal and other viral diseases. The Family Welfare Programme is also an indirect nutrition programme since by reducing family size, it will not only increase the per capita availability of food but also result in better all-round facilities, including health care.

A unique approach to improve child survival, child nutrition and child development is the

Integrated Child development services. started in selected parts of the country about a decade ago, it offers a package of services aiming at all-round child improvement.

Several direct nutrition intervention programmes have been in operation for several years, long enough to have made an impact. The rationale behind these programmes and their effectiveness are briefly presented here.

Special nutrition programme

Started in the early 1970s, this programme aims at the control and prevention of childhood protein-energy malnutrition in the age group 1 to 5 years. free food supplements are given, usually of the ready-to-eat type. Children in the urban slum and the tribal areas are primary targets. The amount of food given is approximately equal to the shortfall between what the child needs and what it actually cats at home. As far as possible, the food supplements is prepared using locally available food stuffs. The food is given for not less than 200 days in the year.

Mid-day meal programme

Initially started in Tamil Nadu, and later taken up by a few other states, this is meant for school children. A complete meal is served in the afternoon. The aim is to improve nutritional status, increase school enrolment, reduce school dropouts and create nutrition-awareness among the children and parents.

Vitamin A prophylaxis programme

This intervention aims at reducing blindness due to vitamin A deficiency among to 5 year old children. All rural, tribal and urban slum children at risk are given a very large single dose-200,000 units of vitamin A in syrup form once every six months. The vitamin A is distributed through the existing primary health care system. This programme was started in 1972, and was based upon extensive studies done in the country earlier, which established the fact that vitamin A deficiency blindness could be eliminated through this simple, inexpensive procedure. several million children are covered under this programme.

Anaemia prophylaxis programme

initiated over ten years ago, the purpose of this programme is to reduce anaemia in two selected high-risk groups-pre-school children and pregnant and lactating women. Tablets containing iron and folic acid are given to pregnant women during the last 100 days of pregnancy, to lactating women during the first six months and to children for 100 days in a year. The dose is one tablet a day. This programme like the Vitamin A prophylaxis programme is operated through the primary health care network.

Goitre control programme

Common salt to which iodine is added is made available in areas which have goitre, with the aim of reducing the number of people with goitre as also to bring down the extent of iodine deficiency disease. The ability of iodized salt to control goitre has been established the world over.

Integrated child development

Started a little over ten years ago in select areas, the ICDS has now been expanded to cover over on-half of the country. Child protection and child development are the central objectives. The package of services include; (i) health check-up of children, pregnant and lactating womens, (ii) immunization; (iii) supplementary feeding of children, pregnant and lactating women; (iv) medical referral service; (v) non-formal education to pre-school children, and (vi) health and nutrition education to mothers. Children from birth to 6 years of age are included. The services are delivered through the 'anganawadi' as the focal point.

An evaluation of these programmes

A common remark in the evaluation of these programmes is their tardy implementation and lack of adequate supervision during implementation. Wherever they have been properly implemented, the anticipated improvements have occurred. Unfortunately such 'success' areas are few.

Child survival programmes are important in the context of bringing down population growth; but if, concurrently, child development programmes are not implemented, there may soon comes time when the nutritional status may become worse than what it is now because of interesting numbers of survivors who do not have an opportunity to grow and develop optimally. The child development component has not received the same emphasis in the country as has the child survival effort.

Improving the nutrition of people is vital for improving the health of the nation and for national development. This can be achieved, not in isolation, but as part of a well-implemented package of services which includes all aspects of socio-economic well-conceived development.

Evaluation of nutrition programmes

S.No. Programme	*Findings*
1. Special nutrition programme	some reduction in the severe forms of malnutrition. Total impacts is much less than-expected
2. Mid-day meal programme	Has not achieved its nutritional and educational objectives
3. Vitamin A prophylaxis programme	Has reduced vitamin A deficiency signs only in patches. Impact is less than expected
4. Anaemia prophylaxis programme	Has had virtually no impact
5. Goitre control programme	Has failed to make any significant impact in many areas
6. Integrated child development services	Some impact on immunization status as also nutritional status of children. Child mortality rates reduced. disappointing with respect to others.

1. A large section of India's population is malnourished, not merely because of economic reasons,but also because of lack of knowledge about food and nutrient needs as well as wrong feeding practices due to food beliefs, and food taboos. This is particularly true during periods of sickness. Though all segments of the population are affected, infants, young children and pregnant and lactating women are especially at risk and constitute the vulnerable groups.

2. Malnutrition contributes substantially to infant and child mortality in the country. This has several demographic repercussions. It increases birth rate and child turnover rate which remote large families. It shortens inter-pregnancy interval and generally discourages the adoption of the small family norm. It also increases the proportion of child population, thus straining the country's limited resources, since children form a large vulnerable group.

3. Family size has a perceptible influence on food intake and nutritional status, particularly of women and children. There are more malnourished subjects among large families than among small families. Also, children with birth orders of four and above, have twice as much malnutritions as do children whose birth orders are three or below. Women who have had more than three pregnancies are more malnourished than are women with fewer pregnancies. Malnutrition in the country can

come down by over 60 per cent, if families restrict the number of children to two or three, even if nothing else is done.

4. The consequences of childhood malnutrition are far reaching. They include impaired physical and mental development, which persist in adult life leading to small adult body size, reduced work capacity and productivity, low earning power and low quality of life. All these perpetuate malnutrition. Its consequences in young girls include unsatisfactory reproductive performance and sub-optimal child rearing when they become adults.

5. Malnutrition limits fertility. This is contrary to the general belief that malnutrition promotes it. It limits fertility by reducing the population sex ratio through more female deaths during infancy and childhood, as also more maternal deaths during the reproductive period. prolonged lactation, which is practiced extensively by poor malnourished communities, also contributes by delaying the resumption of menstruation and prolonging the inter-pregnancy interval. Menarche is delayed by malnutrition, but has little role in influencing fertility.

6. Four nutritional disorders are of public health concern in the country-protein-energy malnutrition, vitamin A deficiency, anaemia and iodine deficiency. They contribute significantly to mortality and ill-health; they

also lead to deficits in physiological functional. The several nutrition programmes both direct and indirect, which have been in operation for quite some time, have made only a-marginal impact, mainly because of poor implementation.

7. All child-survival programmes in the country are linked to child-development programmes, but the latter have not received the same attention and emphasis as the former. if this situation is not rectified, there may soon be a time when the nutritional status may get worse than it is now, simply because of an expanding surviving pool of malnourished individuals.
8. Improvement of nutrition is vital in improving the health of the nation and for national development. This can be achieved not in isolation, but only as part of an integrated package of activities which includes all aspects of socio-economic development.

7 World Population Growth

We shall discuss here population growth and its impact on social behaviour and finally on the eco-system. We will also analyse the impact of factors like (a) Urbanization (b) Crowding on our environment.

One of the major areas of interest and concern for ecology is the scientific study of population. This includes the analysis of population structure and composition, population growth patterns, the natural control of population, and the interaction between population of man, animals and other organisms.

Population studies are fundamental to many human problems in agriculture, pest control, wildlife management, and economic planning. The purpose of population research is to understand the interplay of factors influencing population range, and ultimately to predict and regulate the course of populations. Man obviously wants to limit or reduce populations of organisms, whereas he has wish to maximize within reasonable limits valuable and productive animals for aesthetic or economic reasons. The greatest challenge of all, as well as scientifically and philosophically the most difficult are of human endeavor is understanding and regulation human population change.

Population alarm

The world population was almost stationary during Stone Age, an estimated 10 million people. Sometime between 8000 B.C. and 6000B.C. man learnt the art of growing food, and so could support a large population. As a result the human population increased 50 times in 7000 to 9000 years.

In the next two centuries the population doubled and reached an amazingly high figure of one billion. It took just 100 years to double the population to reach four billion in 1975.

Alarmingly, in 12 years it reached the five-billion mark on July 11, 1987. At the present rate of growth we will add another billion in the next 12 years, unless drastic measures are taken. The present world population of 5.43 billion, which is growing at the rate of 97 million people per year will touch 8.5 billion by the year 2025. About 95% of the population growth will be in the developing countries. At present we add about 500 million people in about six years times, a figure which took thousand of years to reach before 1950 AD.

About 3,42,000 babies are born every day in the world and about 1,5,000 persons die, leaving a net increase of 2,07,000. Thus within a week's time there will be nearly 1.5 million more people. The UN population Fund in a recent report says that in the next 10years there will be one billion more people on Earth, making a total of 6.4 billion. That means another China to house, a million more consumers to feed, house, clothes, and educate.

Trends in population growth

There is no doubt in the fact that human population are drastically out of balance. For thousands of years prior to the seventeenth century, the population of the world was less than 500 million people. Human population were limited by high mortality and even in the great civilizations of Egypt, Greece and Rome, expectation of life probably did not exceed 30 years. The class checks on human population were disease, famine and war. In the fourteenth century, at least 25 percent of the adult population of Europe died in epidemics of bubonic plague and between the years 1348 and 1379 A.D. England's population was reduced almost 50 percent, Cholera, typhus, small pox, malaria yellow fever and sleeping sickness have all been among the great killers of man throughout history. Several of these diseases, especially malaria and yellow fever, severely limited the abundance and distribution of people in tropical countries until the advent of modern medicine and public health.

Asia has traditionally been the great stage for famine though starvation; death also occurred in Europe. The famous Irish famine of 1850 resulted in the death of more than 12 percent of the adult population between 1846 and 1851. In China, in 2000 years preceding the 20th Century, over 1800 separate famines were recorded, many of them killing million of individuals. More recently, 4 million famine deaths occurred in China in 1920-21 more than 5 million is Russia from 1918 to 1923; and over 2 million in India in 1943. Almost agriculture and transportation have alleviated famine mortality, malnutrition continue to be significant demographic for, particularly since it accentuates illness and mortality from infectious disease.

War has also been a major mortality factor throughout history,not only by causing direct battle casualties, but also by stimulating disease and famine. Great epidemics and massive crop failures, have often been triggered by the disruptive condition of warfare. The casualties of war have frequently involved as many civilians as soldiers. Some historians believe that the Thirty year war in Europe between 1618 and 1648 resulted in the death of 30 percent of the inhabitants of Germany and Bohemia.

Despite the combined action of disease, famine and warfare, several major development in the sixteenth, seventeenth and eighteenth centuries stimulated population growth and eased the heavy mortality burdens of man. The opening of the New World provided a vast new area of space and nature resources of economic exploitation. The industrial revolution greatly increased the productivity and control of infectious diseases. The industrial revolution greatly increased the productivity and mobility of man. These factors combined to accelerate human population growth and the world population curve began to rise upward.

The following table indicates the populations growth rates

Region	Population (billions)			% Annual Growth rate		
	1985	2000	2025	1950-85	1985-2000	2000-2025
WORLD	4.8	6.1	8.2	1.9	1.6	1.2
Africa	0.56	0.87	1.62	2.6	3.1	2.5
Asia	2.85	3.55	4.54	2.1	1.6	1.0
Latin America	0.41	0.55	0.78	2.6	2.8	1.4
North America	0.26	0.30	0.35	1.3	0.8	0.6
Europe	0.49	0.51	0.52	0.7	0.3	0.1
U.S.S.R.	0.28	0.31	0.37	1.3	0.8	0.6
Oceania	0.02	0.03	0.04	1.9	1.4	0.9

(Source: Our common Future, 1987.)

Between the birth of Christ and the seventeenth century, the world's population took approximately 1600 years to double. The next doubling as achieved within 200 years, and the next from 1 to 6 million people within 80 years, from 20 to 4 million people were completed by 1975 a span of 45 years and at the current rates of growth the world population will double again within another 35 years.

Currently the world's population is increasing at approximately 2 percent per year—a net increase of about 1,300,000 per week. Every day of every week, the world's population increases by more the 207,000 people. All this is primarily a product of man's increased life span a reduced mortality through modern medicine and agriculture. Man's fertility patterns were basically established during periods of much higher mortality rates thousands of years ago and they have remained high in the intervening year.

Global Distribution:

The developing countries least able to afford rapid population growths are experiencing the greatest growth. The population is not evenly distributed around the world. More than half the world's population regions of the total world, i.e. Europe, North America, former USSR and Oceania had only about 22% of the total world population in mid 1988. The remainder was distributed in the developing region of the world.

The growth rate is most rapid in Africa. In the coming decade, the population there will rise from 640 million to 950 million and it will be the highest regional growth rates the world has ever known. According to projection, countries like Ethiopia, Nigeria, Zaora and Kenya will double their populations within the next 20 years. In North Africa the growth rates are slower, but th figures are still rising fast.

South Asia and Africa together will account for over half of the increase.

Southern Asia's population will rise from 1.2 to 1.6 million. In Eastern Asia the population growth rates have declined rapidly in the past decade, but the number will still increase from 1.3 to 1.5 million people.

Several Arab countries have very high population growth rates and the 12 countries in West Asia will increase in their population to 131 million by 2001.

The population; of Latin America and the Caribean is projected to increase by 100 million from 440 to 540 million. In Central and South America, most countries have annual growth rates in excess of 2%.

Dependency ratio

In addition to the large concentration of population in developing countries, the percentage of population under 15 years and over 64 years of age what is called the dependency ratio is also very high. The population under 15 year is about 45% in Africa, 35% in Asia and 39% in latin America, whereas it is only about 23% in North America 22% in Europe and 29% in Oceania. However, the percentage of population over 64 year is higher in the developed regions of the world. North America has about 11% of its population over 64 years. Europe has about 13% and Oceania about 8%. It is only 3% in Africa and 4% in Asia and latin America.

The high dependency ratio in the developing countries means that age group between 15-64 has to support a large population with requirements for housing, clothing, education, health and other social service. The large young population in developing countries also has demographic implications in the near future.

Asia and Africa, and the regions which will account for about 75% of the world's population in the next 35 years or so, and will have the greatest proportion of poor people. In South Asia 51% of the population lives below the poverty line and in sub Saharan Africa 45% Malnutrition, ill-health, illiteracy and the lowest life expectancy, accompanied by inadequate technology and economic poverty, are predominant in South Asia and Africa. It is not very difficult to imagine the miserable plight of the people in their regions in the next century.

The UNEP has warned that continuing high population growth will result in continuing poverty and increasing environment damage and will lead to higher levels of urban growth and international migration. The population report support this that it will be impossible to keep pace with population trends. If the population growth continues as expected, it says within 10 years there will be more than 200 million children who will receive no education.

What does this mean in terms of human welfare and environment quality? It usually means that many countries have excessive demands for products and services which cannot be met. It is exceedingly difficult, if not impossible, for those countries with the highest rates of population growth to meet the requirements of their people for food, housing, jobs and the physical amenities of life, and it is virtually impossible for them to maintain adequate services in education, medicine, public health and social welfare. Thus we emerge with such problems: (1) 60 percent of the world's people are still inadequately fed, receiving a percapita calorie, intake less than that recommended by the UN (2) 80 percent cf the children of India shows evidence of malnutrition; (3) there are only 9 acres of land surface available for every person on the earth, and only 26 percent of this is available for agricultural production; thus only 1.2 acres of potential cropland are currently available for each person and this is decreasing each year (UN States of Hunger Report); (4) many countries, especially in Asia and Africa, still have an illiteracy rate exceeding 70 percent; (5) in many developing nations, there is only one physician for every 5,00 to 10,00 people, a ratio which makes adequate medical care impossible.

This list could be extended considerably to indicate that many parts of the world are currently living under severe population pressure. While the western nation gain strikingly in prosperity, most of the world's people face increasing poverty and population pressure.

When to global picture is considered, the outstanding fact exists that we can not provide a quality life or maintain a quality environment for the majority of the world's people at the present time, let alone provide for more than 1,600,000 new people every week.

Ecologically, this represents a highly unstable condition, it cannot persist indefinitely without major corrective or compensating changes. These grim facts coupled with increasing global communication, rapid social and technological change and rising expectations throughout all nations add fuel to the fire of social and political instability. As noted by Eric Hoffer in The Ordeal of Change (1963):

"...... a population subject to drastic change is a population of misfits-unbalanced, explosive, and hungry for action. In other words, drastic change under certain conditions, creates a proclivity of fanatical attitudes, united action, and spectacular manifestation of fluting and defiance. It creates on atmosphere of revolution.

The next decade may decide the future of the earth as hesitation for humans. Already our impact has been sufficient to degrade the soil of millions of hectares to thin the ozone layer threatening the rain-forests and to initiate global warming the full consequences of which cannot yet be calculated. At some point in the not too distant future the changes in the environment may cross the threshold of catastrophe.

Again we see the intimate relationships between ecology and human affairs. It does not imply that ecology can provide the answers to all these problems but surely a failure to recognize their ecology background invites certain disaster.

Indian's population situation

India's population, as on March 1, 1992 stood at 843.93 million(437.60 males and 406.33 million females). The second largest population country, India is now the home of 16 percent of world's population. With this, every sixth person in the world is now an Indian. The country however accounts for 2.42 percent of the total world area.

Population counts in India in the modern sense started in 1881 since then, a population census has been conducted regularly every ten years. A census of population was conducted during 1871-72 but it was nosynchrononus. Moreover, the 1972 census omitted served territories, the population of which totaled some 33 million in 1881.

The population of India as recorded at each decade census form 1901 has grown steadily except for a decreased during the decade 1911-21. In absolute terms the country population has increased by 160.60 million from 680.3 million in 1981 to 843.9 million in 1991. This is ten times the population of Australia and is more than the population of Japan.

An encouraging feature revealed by the census result is the decline in the growth rate of the population in the last decade compared to 1971 to 1981. It marginally decreased from 24.66 percent recorded in 1971-81 to 23.50 per cent during 1981-91.

In most state the growth rate declined during the decade. However, Andhra Pradesh, Arunachal Pradesh, Madhya Pradesh, Maharashtra, Nagaland, Jaipur, West Bengal, Daman and Diu, Lakshadweep and Pondicherry which account for one third of the country's population recorded increase in growth rate. Nagaland registered the highest growth rate of the 56.86 percent while Kerala registered the lowest 13.98 percent.

Uttar Pradesh continues to be largest state population wise with 16.44 percent people of the country living there (138,760,417), followed by Bihar with 10.32 percent (86,338,853) and Maharashtra with 9.33 percent (78,706,719). West Bengal occupied fourth place accounting for 80.06 percent (67,982,732) of the country's population followed by Andhra Pradesh with 7.86 percent (66,304,854) Bombay continued to be most populated city of the country with urban population of 12.57 million, Calcutta taking the record place having 10.86 million, Delhi ranks third with a population (urban) of 8.38 million followed by Madras 5.36 million.

Population density

One of the important indices of Population concentration is the density of population. It is defined as the number of person per square kilometer. The population density has gone up from 216 in 1891, to 267 person in 1991. In 1901 it wâs 77 person. Density is the highest in Delhi (6.319) followed by Chandigarh (5,620). Lakshadweep which has the smallest population size is the third most densely populated area with a density of 1,615 person per square kilometer , Pondicherry ranks fourth (1605) followed by Daman and Diu (906) Arunachal is the most sparsely populated area with a density of 1,615 person per sq kilometer. The ten heavily populated districts of the country are Calcutta Madras, Greater Bombay, Hyderabad, Delhi, Chandigarh, Maoe, Haora, Kanpur City and Banglore. All of them have density of above 2,00 person per sq km and 5.0 percent of the country's population lives in these districts. The average density of these 10 districts. The average density of these 10 districts is 5,791.

Sex ratio

In any study of the population, analysis of the sex composition plays a vital role. The sex composition of the population is affected by the differentials in the mentality conditions of males and females, sex relative migration and the sex ratio at birth.

Table: *Sex Ratio (Females per 1,000 Males) in India, 1901-1991*

Census year	*Sex ratio*
1901	972
1911	964
1921	955
1931	950
1941	945
1951	946
1961	941
1971	930
1981	934
1991	929

The sex ratio is defined as the number of females per 1000 males. In India it has generally been adverse to women. The ratio has also declined over the year except in 1981 when it slightly improved to 934 from 930. In 1991, there has been a fall by five points to 929 per 1000 males. But Kerala represented a different spectrum. The State has a higher number of females than males, 1040 females for 1000 males.

In Indian context, a sex ratio of 950 or above can be considered as favorable to females.

The states and Union Territories coming under this category besides Kerala are Himachal Pradesh (96), Andhra Pradesh (972) Goa (969) Karnataka (960) Manipur (961) Orissa (972) Tamil Nadu (972) Dadar & Nagar Haveli(953), Daman & Diu (972) and Pondicherry (982) Chandigarh accounted for lowest number of females per 1000 with 793.

Demographic transition in India

Many scholars have inferred from the actual experience of several European countries and the United States of America that populations historically pass through different more or less well-defined stages in terms of their levels of fertility and mortality. As a generalized explanation of process of mortality and fertility decline in those countries, the transition theory refers to a stage of high fertility in those countries, the transition theory refers to a stage of high fertility and high mortality in simple, mostly agarian, societies which finally transforms itself to a condition of low fertility and low mortality after passing through several other stages. Today the transition theory it sought to be equally applicable to the less developed counties which are still in the early stages of demographic change. In effect this theory has come to be increasingly regarded as theory that might anticipate the future demographic trends in countries which are currently having high population growth due to rapidly decreasing death rate and high but more or less stable or only slowly declining birth rate. Although there are several expositions of demographic transition theory, but the one dividing the total period into five stage is more commonly used. These stages are as below;

(a) The high stationary stage characterised by high birth rates and high death rates;

(b) The early expanding stage with high birth rates but declining death rates;

(c) The late expanding stage with falling death rates but more rapidly falling birth rates;
(d) The declining stage with low mortality now natality and deaths exceeding births.

The first stage which is characterised by agrarian low income economy is marked by relatively stable birth rate at the maximum fertility level found in societies not using contracepitives, and the death rate is found to fluctuate in response to conditions of prosperity or famines, epidemics and other disasters. Then, as the economy progresses to become more interdependent specialised and market dominated with the generation of agricultural surplus, the average death rate begins to decline under the impact of better organisation and improved medical knowledge and care; however, the birth rate continues to remain almost stable at the earlier level. This leads to an increasing growth rate of population which is the early expanding stage. As the death rate continues to decline with further improvements in living conditions birth rate also starts declining first slowly and somewhat later at a faster speed making the 'late expanding stage'. In this stage the growth rate starts getting smaller and smaller than what it was in the early expanding stage. In the fourth stage when further reduction in death rate becomes harder to attain, the death rate stabilizes at a low level (between 8-12 per 1000 persons), the birth rate as approaches equality with the death rate and a more gradual growth rate is established when both birth and death rates are low but birth rate fluctuates some what from year to year in response to voluntary decisions of the people. In the last stage of demographic transition which started to appear in recent years in a few European countries like Germany, Sweden, Switzerland etc., the birth rates has declined even below the replacement level and there may not be enough people in the next generation to replace the present one.

For India, we now have a history of around 100 years of changes in birth and death rates.

Table: Birth and Death Rates in India from 1891-1901 to 1989

Year	Birth rate	Death rate
1891-1901	48	48
1901-1911	49	49
1911-1921	49	49
1911-1931	47	37
1931-1941	45	33
1941-1951	43	31
1951-1961	44	26
1961-1971	42	20
1971-1981	37	15
1980	33.7	12.6
1981	33.9	12.5
1982	33.8	11.9
1983	33.7	11.9
1984	33.9	12.6
1985	32.9	11.8
1986	32.6	11.1
1987	32.2	10.9
1988	31.5	11.0
1989	30.5	10.2

The first stage of demographic transition in India continued till about 1920 when both death rates and birth rates were high. This stage was also marked by purely agrarian economy with hardly any significant industrialisation. High mortality levels were hardly and for the variable growth rates of the population during the 30 or more years before 1921.

A severe famine affected large areas of the country in 1896 and 1897. In the Bombay Presidency (excluding the princely states) especially, the effects of the famine were aggravated by a severe plague. As a result of the two scourges, the 1901 census recorded a population loss of about 2 percent from the 1891 level of 18.8 million.

Like the 1891-1901 decade the next decade also witnessed several local famines and a severe one in 1907 in most parts of Uttar Pradesh. Plague was in evidence in the Bengal and Bombay Presidencies, and both plague and malaria were widespread in the Punjab and Uttar Pradesh where population growth was negligible. Yet, because the country as a whole suffered from famines less widely and for shorter durations, there was an appreciable rise in the population growth rate compared to the previous decade.

During the 1911-20 decade India suffered from an influenza epidemic that caused an estimated 7 percent of the total population to die and led to an absolute decline in the population of the Indian Republic (according to the present boundaries) by 0.77 million at the 1921 census.

The second phase of demographic transition in the country started with the beginning of the 1920s and has spread well up to 1971. This is also the period when industrialization began in the country and took some roots. During this period the major causes of high mortality-famines and epidemics-have been gradually brought under control and between 1921 and 1951, the country witnessed a gradual rise in population growth rates. The decline in death rate became sharper during the 1950s without any appreciable decline in birth rate resulting in a population growth rate of 1.96 percent per annum during 1951-61 in comparison to 1.25 percent during 1941-51 decade. During1961-71 the birth rate still remained quite high and due to further decline in death rate the growth rate increased to 2.05 percent.

India seems to have entered the third stage of demographic transition since 1971 when birth rates has also started declining. During the birth rate leading to a plateau in the population growth rate during the 1960s and the 1970s. In the 1980s, probably the decline in birth rates was slightly greater than that in mortality; consequently the growth rate during this period is slightly lower than in the previous decade.

It is now hoped that there would be faster declines in birth rate than in death rate in the next couple of decades. It is also hoped that India will be at the point by about 2020 if not earlier.

Urbanization

Only one in ten people lived in cities when the century began more than half will by the century's end. Today the vast bulk of urban population growth occurs in developing countries. The populations of Third World cities, now doubling every 10-15 years, overwhelm government's attempts to provide clean water, sewage, adequate transport and other basic services. Cities in

Industrial countries are gaining people much more slowly, yet even as their growth rates slow or core population decline, these urban areas continue to spread out ward. Industrial and developing countries alike, chaotic, uncontrolled urban growth-whether measured is risking numbers or in the amount of space humans spread out upon—draws on ever more land, water and energy from surrounding regions to meet people's needs. The way cities physically evolve—and the way their development is planned has profound impact on human either recognize the limits of the natural environment or it can destroy the resources on which current and future societies depend, it can meet people's needs equitably or it can enrich some while impoverishing or endangering others. The world needs an urban planning ethic that is sensitive to these environmental and human dimensions.

According to 1981 census, India's urban population was 160 million ranking fourth among the countries in the world in terms of absolute size of the urban population, the first three being China, U.S.S.R. and U.S.A. Though the level of urbanization measured as the percentage of urban to total population has increased from 11 percent in 1901 to only 23 percent in 1981 the number of people living in urban areas and multiplied six folds during the period from 26 million, constituting more than one third of the country's population of 926 million at that time.

The growing chaos in urban areas are due to rapid immigration rather than natural increase. A total of 15.7 million persons have migrated from rural to urban areas in the country during the decade 1971-81. The immigrants in the reverse direction i.e. urban to rural numbered. 6.4 million giving rise to a net addition of 9.3 million people in urban areas. There are 218 class I cities in India with more than a lakh population each and these account for about 60 per cent of urban population. Among these, there are 12 metropolitan cities viz., Calcutta (9.16m), Greater Bombay (8.22m), Delhi 5.7m), Madras (4.27), Bangalore (2.9m), Kanpur (1.68m), Pune (1.68m), Nagpur (1.29m), Lucknow (1.0m) and Jaipur (1.0m).

With the data on class I cities and the emergence of new towns on the eve of the 1991 census, we can examine the likely level of urbanization in India. It is well known that the share of Class I urban population has constantly agglomerations and cities in the total urban population has constantly increased over time. If one looks at the total urban population has constantly increased over time. If one looks at the trend in India (excluding Assam) from 1951 to 1981, this share increased from 44.7 per cent to 60.8 per cent, the increase being 6.8 per cent during the 1970s. The increase in the share was higher during the 1950s since a very large a number of small towns (857 in all) were declassified on the eve of the 1961 census due to introduction of a restrictive definition of urban areas.

In contrast, there was a net addition of 895 towns (or 782 urban agglomerations and towns) between 1971 and 1981 which involved reclassification of almost 250 towns declassified on the eve of the 1961 census. Addition of a large number of small and medium towns during the 1980s brought down the pace of increase in the share of population of Class I cities in 1981. As the number of new towns indentified on the eve of the 1991 census is quite large, one may expect a substantial increase in the population of medium and small towns in 1991. If, however, a large number of them appear as part of urban agglomerations of Class I cities, their population will be counted as population of Class I cities. An examination of the list of new towns and of cities and urban agglomerations indicate that a large number of new urban settlements have appeared as part of urban agglomerations. Accordingly, we may expect the share of the population at 65 per cent. This is in view of the fact that 80 Class I cities have been added during the 1980s. We may also not forget that the decadal growth rate of Class I cities slightly declined over the decade compared to the previous decade.

Assuming that the proportion of population of Class I cities in the total urban population of 1991 is 65 per cent, we get the total urban population as 213 million excluding that the Assam and Jammu and Kashmir. If we add the 1991 population of Class I cities of Assam, the estimate of total urban population would remain at the 1981 level (that is, 60.5 per cent), the 1991 urban population (excluding Jammu & Kashmir) works out to 230 million, almost the same as projected by the Expert Committee on Population projections in

1984. Thus, the urbanization rate in 1991 varies between 25.6 per cent to 27.5 per cent.

Keeping in view that the number of metropolises has increased from 12 in 1981 to 23 in 1991, and that the number of Class I cities has increased from 216 to 296 during the same period, one may expect a higher share of Class I cities in the total urban population than 65 per cent. If this is found to hold good when the data on rural and urban population are released, the total urban population would be less than 214 million.

Population in the twentieth century has exploded particularly in the developing countries. Infact, before 1800, no country was predominantly urban. But by the year 2000, over 50 per cent of the world's population will probably live in urban places and there will probably be more than 250 cities of over one million inhabitants.

There has been a world wide trend towards urbanization, the process characterized by the movement of people from rural to urban settlements, from small towns to large cities, and from large cities to the suburbs. This immigration is caused by and in turn leads to profound societies change. Rural areas are depopulated, while urban areas towns, cities and urban zones—become more densely populated. Since most of the cities are growing in an unplanned way there arises a number of problems such as housing, traffic, shortage of open space & pollution.

Problem of Housing

The Indian cities are growing both vertically (multi-storey building culture) and horizontally (invasion of the peripheries). In spite of cities expansion there is growing shortage of house (3.8m), growth of slums and squatter settlements, creating interpersonal and intercity imbalances, breaking down services and acceutuation of the problem of urban renewal. Slums are now becoming permanent features and are proliferating and sheltering larger population every year. They are having small tenements, narrow lanes, lack of sanitation, water supply, electricity, unhygienic environment, etc. Due to realization of the futility of spending money on their clearance, the Government had decided to accord them recognition and gave their residents whatever amenities the funds allowed. Bombay is estimated to have the largest slum population of 3.3 m followed by Calcutta 3.2m, Delhi 2.6m, and Madras 1.8m. With an unabated inflow of job seekers, these cities are expected to see continuing rise in their slum population. By 1990 when Calcutta will have a population of 12.5m and its slum will be harboring 4.4m Madras population will be 11.8m, 9.7m and 6.0m and of them 4.1, 3.1 and 2.1m slum dwellers.

Amongst States, Uttar Pradesh will have the largest slum population of 6.5m followed by Maharashtra 6.2m, West Bengal 4.9m, Tamil Nadu 4.2m, by the end of the decade. The Government's initial strategy was to clear the slums and rehabilitate their dwellers. This had to be given up by the end of the sixth plan as there was constant shortage of funds and developed land. The emphasis was shifted to an on going central scheme known as "Environmental Improvement of Urban Slums," envisaging a package of services for the immediate removal of unhygienic environment of the slums. The services included drinking water, community bathrooms, street-lighting, sewerage, storm water drains and street paving.

Traffic Problems

The traffic problem in urban areas is one of the greatest problems of the day. Most of the cities and towns are growing in unplanned way. Due to lack of proper enforcement agencies encroachment in all parts of the cities is going rapidly and due to political interference, authorities become in competement. Most of the roads are narrow, haphazard and ill-maintained. Traffic problem is getting bad to worse because of high density of population desire to have personal means of transport and to live near the city, mixed traffic, lack of civic sense, ill-maintained road, inadequate expansion in the existing road network poor regulation of traffic, etc. Delhi had 12,000 vehicles in 1951 and the number had shot upto 9 lakh in 1986 and this is expected to reach 40 lakh by 2001. Apart from the fast moving vehicular traffic, the problem on the city roads is being further aggravated because of 50,000 or more slow moving vehicles such as tongas, rickshaws and bullock carts and 20 lakh cycles. There is also a growing trend of road accidents. There were 6,037 reported road accidents of which 1,162 persons lost their lives in 1986. According to National Transportation Planning and Research Centre, Trivandrum in every four minutes there is one road accident in India, killing or injuring one person on an average.

Shortage of Open Space

Due to increasing commercial value of the land in cities, open spaces are diminishing, even though green spaces are the lungs of the cities, the guarantors of a healthy and aesthetic environment. In Japan, urban parks are classified under two main categories; parks with structures or city parks and zoned green spaces, which are further subdivided into green space conservation zones, agricultural green space and special historical land space zones/scenic beauty conservation zones. City park land includes playgrounds, open spaces, planting strips along side road and other lands awaiting full development.

It is commonly said that these parks become the pursuit of undesirable activities including sex, crime, gambling, etc. In spite of these negative aspects, it provides thousand times much needed benefits for the city dwellers.

There is a concept to have at least 20 per cent area of the cities under open space in the form of green belts, parks, playgrounds, etc. But it has become an utopian concept. In 1973, master plan of Allahabad was approved and much of the areas were put under green belts. But due to illegal spraw of colonies most of that very areas were converted into concrete belts. The green belts concepts are also not getting proper place in the city environment improvement scheme because of lack of financial support, public interest and professionally qualified staff. Besides this, there is not definite framework for parks and recreational areas in relation to national goals. City parks and green belts are developed mostly by Municipalities or Corporations, Social Forestry and Horticulture departments. Private organizations, voluntary organizations, industries should also come forward to set city parks and green belts. Vacant lands acquired by the Corporation are to be sued not only for commercial or residential settlement but also for establishing big parks. Local communities must come forward to participate in the management of parks and can also raise funds for it. Country parks can be established in rural areas to provide a better place for recreation and enjoyment of rural people. In addition to parks and gardens, landscaping measures should be applied on flyovers, overhead bridges, wall and other structures, such as the growing of creepers, climbers, scrubs and transplanted trees. There is a need for making legislation for City and Country Parks Act for the forceful implementation of the concept of green belt.

Urban Planning Around the Globe

Virtually all cities share some land related concerns, such as congestion and pollution from motor vehicles, lack of affordable housing, and the cancerous growth of blighted district. Of course, prescriptions for better urban planning are not the same for all parts of the world. Many land use issues in industrial countries seem mainly concerned with the quality of urban life, and those in Third World cities are often questions of life and death. But all cities, whether surrounded by affluent suburbs or makeshift shanty towns, now need to plan land use far more carefully than in the past before the developing world's urban crises than into catastrophes, and the industrial world' urban crises turn into catastrophes, and the industrial world's problems become issues of survival.

The extent to which cities control the use of land varies widely. Japan and Western Europe have the world's most comprehensive urban land use controls; their cities are generally compact, laid out for efficiency in transport, water and energy use, and building materials. Japan protects farmland with strict zoning and tax policies. Its suburbs are of moderate, not low, density. Much of Japan's urban activity is concentrated in Tokyo and along the dense Tokadio corridor between that city and Osaka. This compact, linear form has allowed great efficiency in transport, including development of the world's first high-speed train, which has been running since 1964. However, the country's 33 million automobile—nearly twice as many as in all other countries combined—still plague Japanese cities with extreme traffic congestion, especially in the Tokyo area.

Western Europe has a long tradition of activity controlling land use so that the small amount of available space serves the public's interest more than that the private developers. Paris, a city for nearly 2,000 years, has planned and regulated land use since the Middle Ages.

Many of England's urban areas, still fulfilling a far sighted decree by Queen Elizabeth I in 1580, are ringed by green belts intended to protect farmland and prevent sprawl. But in post war decades the automobile has had a profound effect on Europe's compact character, fuelling suburbanization. In the fifties and sixties, some older European cities embraced the U.S. model, demolishing corner shops and cafes to make way for urban freeways. Later, planners tried to contain suburbanization by diverting growth into smaller satellite towns. Since the mid-seventies, they have turned their attention to revitalizing shrinking inner cities.

Control of land use in Eastern Europe and the Soviet Union has not been as effective as might be assumed for centrally planned economies. Urban planning therefore is not well coordinated with economic decisions, and sometimes reflects rivalries among government ministries. Extreme water air, and soil contamination from poor placement and regulation of polluting industries is a critical concern. Although urban planners in these countries historically have supported public transport and promoted urban densities high enough to make it viable, in recent years and use has become less efficient. Nearly all new housing has sprung up at the edges of cities, with few accompanying shops, jobs, or schools, resulting in excessively long commutes. On going political reform and the region's cities will become more automobile-oriented, perpetuating the environmentally destructive patterns of western industrial cities.

Among industrial regions, North America and Australia have the weakest planning traditions. Governments on these continents have done relatively little to guide development beyond separating industrial areas from those zoned for commerce and housing. Many have enforced low-density zoning in an effort to curb urban expansion—a move that, ironically, achieves just the opposite. Zoning codes that restrict residential density, usually by requiring each house to occupy its own large lot, have forced development to consume even greater tracts of open space. And to accommodate new, outlying communities, roads have been extended further outward, attracting even more spread out growth.

Even older U.S. cities are becoming more dispersed now than in the pre-automobile area. Growth in the New York metropolitan region has turned to sprawl; while population has grown only 5 per cent in the past 25 years, the developed areas has increased by 61 per cent—consuming nearly quarter of the region's open space, forest, and farm land. Many people move out to the suburbs and exurbs seeking open space and bounds with nature that come only in a rural setting. Yet most of these residents continue to maintain urban lifestyle—communiting to jobs in the city and demanding urban amenities from a suburban shopping mall near their home. The result is neither urban nor rural living but a destructive compromise that the environment sustain.

Developing countries have the loosest controls over how cities develop. Local governments in Asia,

Africa, and Latin America often have neither the authority to guide land use nor the funds to provide basic services. Municipalities are fiscally dependent on central government, which are themselves struggling under crushing debt burdens. With few exceptions, urban planning is a relatively recent phenomenon in developing countries, even in the capitals. In India it reportedly began with Delhi's Master Plan in 1962. In Nigeria, the first systematic effort to plan cities did not begin until 1971; the capital, Lagos, still has no designated metropolitan government and no formally defined urban area. The Lagos State Ministries that have their own priorities.

The Third World is burdened by several enormous, rapidly growing cities—including-Sao Paulo, Shanghai, and Mexico City—whose sheer size and instability create problems on an entirely different scale. As early as 1964, researcher Ronald Wraith used a single word to denote these giant cities racked with pollution and rimmed by shanty-towns: "Megalopolis-the city running riot with no one able to control it." Since then, megacities have become increasingly characteristic of the developing world. In 1950, only three of the world's 10 largest cities were in the Third World by 1980, seven of them were there.

Although skilled land use planning is badly needed in these megacities, its effectiveness is limited in the absence of other kinds of change. One reason is that most of the physical growth takes place in illegal unplanned squatter settlements, rendering useless even existing mechanisms for guiding land use. Called fevelas in

Brazil bidonvilles in French-speaking West Africa, Spanish in the Middle East, and kampungs in Indonesia, these illegal communities hold 30-60 per cent of the population of many Third World cities. The unhealthy conditions in these settlements can only be addressed fully through extensive economic and social reforms that attack the root causes of poverty not just in cities but also in the rural areas that urban migrants abandon in search of economic opportunity. The effectiveness of land use planning is also limited in the absence of family planning programs. (Only in Africa does migration account for the increase in much of Asia and Latin America results from the fertility of people already in cities). Finally, planners in the Third World's giant cities faces colossal environmental problems, from deadly air pollution in Mexico City, to indiscriminate dumping of toxic wastes in Alexandria, to the actual sinking of cities such as Bangkok, Jakarta, and Shanghai due to over-drawing of ground water.

Crowding

Crowding is a conspicuous ecologic force impinging upon modern man. It results from more than a simple increase in population density. It is also a product of activity patterns psychological needs, and social contact. Crowding implies a force, a pressure and psychological reaction. No clear definition of crowding is possible at the present time; it remains an operational concept with many subjective qualities. Crowded population are, however, easier to recognize than to define, and they are studied more carefully, better definitions may become possible. For the time being, we might define crowded populations as those in which there seem to be excessive number of individuals per unit space in relation of the activity of the industrials and the quality of the environment.

With an operational concept of this type, ecological studies have shown that some rodent populations may be "crowded" in relation to their social behavior and habitual requirement at a density of 5 individuals per acre, where as other at the same species may not be "crowded" until they have a density of several hundred per acre. Species differ in this regard, and so also individuals and social groups within the same species. A western cattle rancher may feel "crowded" at a density of 10 homesteads per square mile whereas a modern suburbanite may feel relatively "uncrowded" at a density of several hundred homes per square mile. The western rancher ranges several square miles per day over what he considers his personal property and he does not welcome potential competitors in his territory. Conversely, suburbanite restricts his daily movements, apart from going to work and to shop, to a lawn around his home, and he does not view neighbors as a competitive threat. Hence, in both animal ecology and human sociology, it is important to distinguish between population density per se, and crowding, since the latter depends so much on behavioral factors.

The spatial requirements of man are obviously very variable, and result from both individual difference and social conditioning. It is impossible to state what the optimal spatial and social needs of man are as those of the Japanese city dweller ar much different than those of the Kansas farmer. Nevertheless, it is safe to assert that man is now subjecting himself to increased crowding through the combined forces of population growth, urbanization, transportation and mass communication.

Man's perception of crowding has skyrocketed upwards in recent years. The growth of urban traffic and the increased number of people in public buildings, schools, hospitals, stores, exhibitions, recreational areas, etc., have all contributed to the feeling of population pressure. Through the mass media or audios, television and newspapers, individuals are vastly more aware of worldwide events. Social pressures at any point of the globe are quickly felt by all nations. Local crime, violence, and warfare now become worldwide worries in a matter of hours. The people of one continent feel threatened by those of another continent thousands of miles away. The inevitable result has been a great magnification of social anxiety and population pressure. The world has thus become more limited in its psychological space, and man more crowded in a social and behavioural sense.

How does one evaluate crowding as an ecologic force? It definitely requires knowledge of at least three major parameters: (1) population density, (2) environmental structure, and (3) social behaviour in relation to each of the possible in both animals and man, but in both, especially man, it is often possible to isolate crowding as the key variable. Many other factor are interwoven. Crowded human populations are often so characterized by poverty, malnutrition, lack of educational and recreational opportunities, varies environmental hazards and unstable social patterns that it is virtually impossible to separate crowding itself as the one key variable. The essential question becomes, how does one measure and analyze crowding per se apart from all it related phenomena? It may also be important to distinguish between crowding of various origins. Since man often seeks social contact and stimulation, does not crowding contain constructive and creative social elements, or is it inevitably a factor in increased social problems and environmental deterioration?

From man himself the answer to these questions are confusing and uncertain. The behavioral sciences of man have just begun to investigate human spatial behavior. More direct clues have come from animal studies where experimental work has been possible. The simpler social systems of many animals have permitted more direct observation of behavior, more ready identification of variable, and more penetrating analyses of causes and effect relationships. In animal studies it has been possible to distinguish between extrinsic crowding; that crowding imposed on the animals as an external force, as in captivity, compared to intrinsic crowding in which dense aggregations result from the social behavior of the animals. A similar distinction is sometimes possible in human populations, but frequently it is difficult to discern if people are crowded by choice or the external pressures of economics and society.

It was demonstrated more than 30 years ago by Professor W.C. Alee and his students of the University of Chicago that most species of animal have optimal levels of crowding, above which and below which deleterious effects occur. These studies showed that certain levels of crowding are necessary to maintain normal biologic function and social activity. Goldfish, for example, grow most rapidly and live longest in social groups of certain densities compared to isolated fish to fish in smaller groups. Fresh water shrimp survive longest and tolerate harmful environmental conditions most successfully at certain optimal stage of crowding. Similarly bobwhite quail survive harsh winters best and reproduce most successfully in the spring in conveys of certain optimal size. Beyond optimal levels of crowding, however, benefits are quickly lost and various forms of pathology, occur. Growth may be stunted, life span shortened and various diseases or abnormal behaviors appear.

Most studies on crowded animal populations in the last 20 years have concentrated primarily on the harmful effects of overcrowding. Such effects usually involve both physiologic and behavioral abnormalities. The physiologic effect of overcrowding centre around endocrine imbalances of the adrenal pituitary system. These imbalances can lead to a great variety of disease condition including gastric ulcers, hypertension, nephrosclerosis, arteriosclerosis, and increased susceptibility of infectious diseases. Prolonged exposure to crowding and its associated stresses have produced additions disease (hypoadrenalism or adrenal exhaustion) myasthenia (muscular weakness), and a variety of serious metabolic disorders leading to shock, coma, and even death. It should be pointed out that these stress effects are quite variable, however, and do not consistently reflected the same patterns in different individuals and various social groups.

Behavioral pathologies also appear in experimental animals as a result of crowding and these are sometimes manifested more quickly than are the physiologic changes. Overcrowded animals often show increased aggression and violence, abnormal sexual behavior, disruption of normal nest building and maintenance, breakup of stable social groups, disappearance of alteration of normal social roles, parental desertion of young and frequently cannibalism of young.

The leading question, of course, is whether or not similar processes occur in man as a result of overcrowding. There are so many variables in man which affect health and behavior, that this becomes a very difficult question. There is no doubt that some striking correlations of disease and behavior are associated with urban concentrations. Many human problems seem to be so accentuated in crowded populations that they virtually constitute an "inner city syndrome" disease, and emphysema; maternal problems such as high prenatal loss, parturitional difficulties and high infant mortlity; behaviour problems such as alcoholism, drug abuse, mental illness, and criminal assault; and social problems such as high divorce rates and social instability.

More recently it has been found that high prevalence of mental illness in the lower socioeconomic classes and dense urban ghettos of several other cities. The three volume report on Manhattan entitled, "Mental Health in Metropolis," also found unusually high prevalence of mental illness in crowded inner city inhabitants.

The problem of urban man seem so strikingly similar to those effects produced in overcrowded animal populations, it is tempting to conclude that similar processes are occurring. But, as stated previously, many factors are interacting with crowding in urban manpower, malnutrition, lack of educational and recreational opportunities, various environmental hazards, and unstable social patterns—that it is virtually impossible to separate cause and effect relationships. There are enough solid exceptions to the principle of "high density produces high pathology" that one must be cautious in carrying this dogma too far. For example, the young nation of Singapore is obviously crowded—over 2,00C,000 people on an island of 224 square miles, making it one of the most densely populated nations of the world—yet it enjoys remarkable good health. The death rate is one of the lowest in the world (5.5 per 1000) and the prenatal mortality is lower than that of Britain and the United States. Major factors in this good record many be its youthful population (40 per cent of the Singapore population is under 15 years of age), and the well planned interspersion of parks and greenbelts with residential and commercial areas. One does not feel a "crowded" in generalizing as in Hong Kong, Tokyo, New York and Calcutta. Such variable demonstrate the difficulty of generalizing broadly about crowding or population density as a pathologic influence. Thus, the precise role of crowding in the "inner city syndrome" must remain a cloudily issue until more and better research studies are available.

An encouraging development of recent years is the awareness on the part of some architects, city planner anthropologist and others of the relationship between our environment and mental health. In Architectural Environment and our Mental health (1968), Moiler explores the impact of physical space and structure on the physiological well-being of man. He noted that more buildings will be built in the next ten years than have accumulated since the beginning of civilization." And he wisely emphasized that, "We should recognize that if we continue to permit the structuring of a physical environment which is essentially hostile, to which man must somehow try to adopt, the cost to individuals and to society will be far too grat—in terms of mental illness, delinquency, poor motivation and fulfillment of our capabilities for creative work and community usefulness."

Anthropologists have also been interested in the spatial behaviour of man, and the book by Professor E.T. Hall (1968) entitled "The Hiddeen Dimension," was the first one to highlight some of the behavior patterns of man relating to social spacing. Hall showed the existence of "personal space" individuals and pointed out cultural differences in the extent and importance of personal space. A book edited by Esser (1971) reviewed the interest of psychiatrists, sociologists, biologists and psychologists, in the relationship of ecology and environment of human behavior. It emphasized how little we know about ourselves in these vital matters.

Although most of the data on human spatial behavior are preliminary, it is a hopeful sign that several professional and scientific disciplines are now giving attention to this topic. We can be assured that the ecology of crowding will become increasingly vital to man's health and welfare.

Appendix

Vital role of census in planning and policy making

The 1991 Census of India should be taken seriously by all and, in particular, by the Central and State governments, for more than one reason. It is just as well that the Eighth Five Year Plan has not yet been prepared and the earlier Approach Paper is being recast. This delay will permit the Planning commission to use at least the first results of the 1991 Census in their planning exercise. The detailed tables, which will be available after some time lag, in spite of the use of electronic computers, should be indispensable in the preparation of the long-term Perspective Plan. It is obvious that neither the Eighth Plan nor the Perspective Plan can be based on obsolete 1981 Census data.

In the context of our Five Year Plans there is now a clear recognition by our politicians and planners that the paramount issue before the country is finding employment for millions of our unemployed and underemployed people. In fact, the political survival of different parties would increasingly depend on the extent to which they can satisfy the voters about their capability to meet the challenge of unemployment, when they come to power. The 1991 Census will give a clear picture of the state of economic activity, the diversification in our industrial structure, if any, since 1981, the magnitude of new entrants to the labour force and the number of persons seeking employment.

Population and employment

It has been recognised by experts and laymen that the unemployment situation has been aggravated by four decades of relentless population growth. India's population problem, is not centred around food but employment. Once can legitimately ask: Why has the population growth rate remained high in spite of India being the first country in the world to have pronounced a state policy of direct intervention through the family planning programme to bring down the birth rate?

In view of the results of the 1991 Census which show a high rate of population growth, the Government of India and the Planning Commission would be compelled to do much more than change the decimal points in their calculations or appoint an expert committee to make projections to calculate the demand for food, housing, education, health, etc. They will have to abandon the status quoist approach to the family planning programme and redesign and not merely revamp the sterile family planning programme which has failed to deliver the goods.

It would be wrong to conclude that the major use of the 1991 Census data will be restricted to the figures for the overall growth rate of the population and, more importantly, to the growth rate of the labour force. There are several other major areas of concern which call for the use of 1991 Census data.

Rapid urbanisation and migration

First and foremost among these other areas is, undoubtedly, the issue of rapid urbanisation and our exploding cities. The National Commission on Urbanisation which was appointed by the then Prime Minister, Mr. Rajiv Gandhi was seriously handicapped by the non-availability of relevant and up-to-date data on various facets of urbanisation. Their major statistical exercise was based, almost entirely, on the 1981 Census data. If the 1991 Census data are imaginatively tabulated or the tapes handed over to concerned urban experts, our urbanisation policies will be better formulated.

A related issue is migration. While it is important to know the quantum of rural-to-urban migration, planners cannot ignore three other migration streams, namely, rural-to rural, urban-to-rural and urban-to-urban. The 1991 Census will present data for all the four migration streams. An improvement in the 1991 Census is with regard to the reasons for migration. The precoded answers to the question on "reasons for migration from place of last residence" at this Census will include two new items; (i) "business" and (ii) "natural calamities like droughts, floods, etc.".

India suffers a tremendous loss, both human and material, on account of natural calamities every year. For the first time, we will now have an idea of the magnitude of "distress migration" caused by natural calamities all over the country.

Housing

Another area of major concern for our planners and policy-makers is housing, both rural and urban. During the houselisting operation for the 1991 Census, data have been collected on the ownership pattern of houses, the type of wall, type of roof, and most important of all, data on availability of water, toilet facilities, etc. In 1981, data regarding toilet facilities were collected only in the urban areas but during the 1991 Census, such data have been collected for rural areas as well. A new question which has been canvassed in the 1991 Census during the houselisting operation is in regard to the type of fuel used for cooking by the household. This will throw valuable light on the consumption of energy. Time and again, attempts are made to formulate a National housing Policy. A population census is not a housing census. Nevertheless, the 1991 Census would provide valuable data on housing and housing infrastructure, right from the aggregate all-India level to the village and individual block level of big cities.

Pensioners

In the Western countries and also in Japan, there is increasing concern for the aging population. An inevitable consequence of a rapid reduction in the fertility level is an increasing proportion in the elderly age groups. The developed countries of the world today are facing a much more serious population problem than the developing countries. It would be simplistic to perceive the population problem only in terms of a high birth rate. A low birth rate also creates serious problems: the proportion of children goes down as a result of the fertility decline and the proportion of the young and the middle-aged population starts increasing, and after a time lag, the proportion of the elderly increases. Care of the elderly in developed countries calls for enormous financial resources because of the high cost of social security and medical care. Even more serious are problems of mental illness, the erosion of family solidarity and cracks in the institution of marriage. The reluctance of voters to put away money for the elderly when the unemployment rate among the young is high gives a political colour to these issues.

The 1991 Census shown some concern for the elderly, at the behest of the Ministry of Defence, by asking a new question on ex-servicemen and pensioners. It would have been more useful if data were sought in regard to all pensioners. In fact, all such data could be collected from Government records. for obvious reasons, the Indian censuses do not collect data on income which some other census do. In the Indian context, it is important to know how to do the old persons survive? What is the source of their income? Who takes care of them? The 1991 Census cannot answer these questions. It must be noted, however, that the Census will collect data on the relationship of each member to the head of the household. If these data are competently tabulated and analysed we will get a valuable picture of the changing Indian family both in urban and rural areas.

Economic census

During the houselisting operation of the 1991 Census, an Enterprise List was canvassed on behalf on the Central Statistical Organisation. This is called the Economic Census and the data were handed over to CSO. THe object was to collect data from every single economic enterprise throughout the country on the type of activity, type of ownership, number of persons employed, power, etc. The quick manual tabulation results of the Economic Census have just been released by the Director General of CSO.

Technical personnel

Finally, we may refer to another important aspect of the Census, namely, collection of data on post-graduate degree holders and technical personnel, through a special questionnaire distributed to all heads of households.

Improvements in the 1991 census

According to the Census Commissioner, the special features of the 1991 Census are as follows.

(1) "The Houselist was expanded to cover some information relating to housing and household amenities which was collected during the main enumeration in 1981. By thus advancing the

collection of this information during house-listing tabulation of data on housing stock and amenities is expected to be completed earlier than last time.

(2) A question was canvassed for the first time through the Houselist regarding type of fuel used for cooking by the household. This will help in knowing the impact of the fuel consumption patterns on environment and forest resources and also reveal the extent to which alternative energy sources are being used for domestic cooking.

(3) In the Houselist, the availability of toilet facility to the household was collected in respect of rural areas also as against only urban areas in the 1981 Census.

(4) The Household Schedule was so designed as to record the data on mother tongue and religion of each individual. This schedule is proposed to be used for the expeditious manual tabulation of the following:

(i) The table called "Primary Census Abstract" with nine-fold industrial categories up to the village level or ward of a town. The basic census data will be presented for the first time for each Community Development Block in the rural areas all over the country, in addition to other levels like Tehsil/Taluka/District/State or Union Territory.

(ii) The mother tongue and religion data upto the Tehsil/Town level. This will help in releasing these tables which are in great demand within a reasonable time after the census taking. Further, this will permit simultaneous commencement of computerised data processing of the individual Slips for other tabulations and cross-tabulations.

(5) A new feature of the individual Slop of ate 1991 Census is that it contains a question on ex-servicemen and their status as pensioner or non-pensioner.

(6) In the 1981 Census, the children in the age group 0-4 were considered as illiterates by definition. At the time of preparation for the 1991 Census, the Department of Education in the Ministry of Human Resource Development and the Planning Commission desired that in the 1991 Census, children in the age group 0-6 should be considered as illiterate since the ability to read and write with understanding is not generally achieved, especially in the rural areas, until a child attaīns the age of 7 or more. Accordingly, in the 1991 Census, children of the age of 6 years or less, were considered as illiterates even if the child was going to school and might have picked up reading and writing a few odd words.

(7) The concepts and definitions relating to economic questions in general and 'work' in particular adopted in the 1981 Census were retained for the sake of comparability. However, sufficient thought was given to the design and formulation of these questions in the Individual Slop. A sub-group of the

Advisory Committee went into this aspect and care was taken to frame the questions in such a way as to help betting' the unpaid workers on farm or in family enterprise. In order to ensure that the economic activity of these categories is properly enumerated in the 1991 Census, the instructions to census enumerators were expanded and emphasis was laid on the need to ask probing questions regarding the work done at any time at all last year or any of the seasons in the reference period, in the case of women. Some of the valuable suggestions made by the women's organisations with regard to completely netting the economic activity of women were taken into account while drafting the instructions to the enumerators and in designing the training modules for them. Special posters supplied by the United Nations Development Fund for Women highlighting the importance of recording women's work were also distributed widely to sensitise the enumerators and the respondents.

(8) In order to provide more detailed tables on the economic activity of the population, it is proposed to process in the 1991 Census all the Individual Slops relating to main workers other than cultivators and agricultural labourers, marginal workers and those non-workers seeking/available for work. In the last census this tabulation was based only on a 20 per cent sample of Individual slops.

(9) The Question on seeking/available for work

was asked in the 1991 Census only in respect of non-workers and not for marginal workers also as was done in the 1981 Census. Further, in case of those seeking/available for work, a question whether they had ever worked before was asked. This will help in knowing the number of fresh entrants to the labour force.

(10) While collecting the information on reasons for migration, two more reasons, namely, 'business' and 'natural calamities like drought, floods, etc.' were added in the 1991 Census by assigning separate codes."

Organising the second largest census in the world

There is hardly any country in the world today 3which does not conduct a population census. A modern population census is much more than a headcount. It is an essential tool in planning and policy-making. Nevertheless, from time to time, questions have been asked about the need for a decennial population census which costs enormous time and money and taxes the administration in charge of the census, particularly in countries like China and India where the census is a monumental affair. Statistically speaking, a well-designed sample can give even better results than a census based on a full count. so why not replace the census by sample surveys?

It may be recalled that India's leading statistician, the late Prof. P.C. Mahalanobis had advised Jawaharlal Nehru, the first Prime Minister of India to introduce National Sample Surveys in 1950. Today, we rely heavily on NSS data in almost all of our planning efforts. Constant efforts are made to improve the quality of NSS data. In 1964, Mr. Asok Mitra, ICS who was the 1961 Census Commissioner, introduced the Sample Registration System throughout the country. Thanks to the vision and dedicated work of Mr. Mitra, we have today a comprehensive decennial population census as well as a yearly sample survey of births and deaths. The main limitation of SRS data, however, is that district wise estimates are not available because of the small size for the sample.

The Planning Commission demands data at the district level and even block level. For monitoring the family planning programme, we need data at the district level but neither the NSS nor the SRS can supply data at the district level, let along at the block level. This is where the census scores over sample surveys. The 1991 Census, for example, will present basic demographic and economic data at the block level. In fact, certain items of census data are available at the individual village level and individual city/town level. But he main limitation of census data lies in the decennial nature of the census though some countries have a five-yearly census. The census cannot provide yearly data except from estimates based on then yearly data.

Census versus sample surveys

Statisticians will argue that if the size of the ample is increased, it is possible to have districtwise estimates of births, deaths and other demographic data. But then the cost of SRS will be enormous. It is unfortunate that the Finance

Ministry has always taken a conservative view of money spent on data collection. For example, when successive Census Commissioners argued that the Indian census is conducted almost FREE by an army of so-called voluntary school-teachers and revenue officials who re increasingly grudging such work, and therefore, a suitable honorarium for the enumerators was necessary, the Finance Ministry pleaded that there was no money. All that the 1991 Census Commissioner could manage was a paltry sum of Rs. 225 for an enumerator for working for three weeks in addition to the period of training. The Census Commissioner is up against an army of demotivated enumerators who are indifferent to their work. 'Will this affect the quality of census'? I ask Mr. Amulya Ratna Nands, the 1991 Census Commissioner. He replies: "I do how we will succeed this time but I doubt if the census can be conducted in 2001, if the Finance Ministry continues to take a conservative view.

The Finance Ministry also talk a conservative view, when in the past, a request was made by the Office of the Registrar General to raise the SRS budget in order to increase the sample. The matter went up to the Cabinet Secretary but nothing was done. It may be noted that the NSS field investigators get a regular salary plus T.A. and D.A. amounting to Rs. 1,500 or so per month wile the 1991 census enumerator would get only rs. 325 for the entire census work. The entire 1991 census operation would cost roughly Rs. 126 crores for the enumeration work and another Rs. 160 crores for data processing tabulation, and analysis and dissemination of data. Thus the total cost of this census would be less than Rs. 300 crores.

The tragedy is that the census is neglected by the Government in spite of the growing demands of the Planning Commission for more data, purely because the head of the census organisation has the rank of a joint Secretary. To my mind, it is absolutely essential to give the rank of a Special Secretary to the Census commissioner and also not transfer him or promote him till the report on the census is written. It may be recalled that the 1961 census report was not prepared because Mr. Asok Mitra was promoted and transferred to another ministry. Likewise, the 1971 and 1981 census reports were also not prepared because the respective census commissioners were transferred and promoted before the census work was completed. One can argue with some justification that there is no need today for the omnibus type of census reports prepared by the British Census Commissioners. I would agree with this viewpoint, provided the census tables are quickly processed and released to the data users. Otherwise the census would fail to deliver the goods.

There is a strong case for setting up a proper research division in the census office. It is absolutely essential to raise the census budget and debit the amount to the Five Year Plans. The present situation is totally unsatisfactory and calls for intervention from the prime Minister who is the Chairman of the Planning Commission. No doubt, Mr. A.R. Nanda is doing a competent job for the conduct of the 1991 census but there are limits to what he can do to induce 1.7 million school teachers and local revenue officials to work free for the government.

Need for census

Let me get back to the question of census versus sample surveys. I ask Mr. N., Rama Rao, Deputy Registrar General, a trained statistician-demographer: "Do you think a census is necessary in India", He replies: "We have no worthwhile system of civil registration for collecting reliable data on births and deaths so that we can make yearly estimates of population growth at any level, say, district or block. We have been relying on the census for estimating births and deaths during the preceding decade. Neither the SRS nor the CRS can substitute for the census in India; we must continue with our census".

I ask Mr. K.K. Chakravorty, a former Deputy Registrar General: "Why are we not able to collect data on births and deaths in spite of the law we enacted in 1969, making the registration of births and deaths compulsory", penalty under this Act for non-registration of births and deaths? It is Rs.10 only and that too is a complicated procedure" Obviously, the Law Ministry did not do its homework properly.

It would be wrong to think that census-taking is a problem only on large countries like China and India. Size of population s not the only problem. On a recent visit to Germany, I asked my demographer friends about the German census. They said: "It has messed up. Many people refuse to co-operate with the census because they feel that the census violates their privacy. There is a lot of litigation against the Government." Besides, Germany has excellent sample surveys and the need for a census is not pressing. I believe a time will come when people will grudge even sample surveys.

In the U.S., where the last census was conducted in 1990, the situation is even worse. I was on a short visit to that country and I could see for myself the growing opposition to the census and the increasing litigation against the Government. People wanted to be left alone. Why should the Government find out the marital status of the people or the age of women? It is worth nothing that the U.S. has an excellent record of decennial population censuses dating back to 1970. The non-response in the initial round of the 1990 U.S. census was so high that the Bureau of Census got perturbed and had to hire enumerators to go round selectively from house to house. But if the U.S. Census Bureau had to hire enumerators to go from house to house all over the country as is done in India, the cost would be so enormous that no census would be taken. On the 1980 Census of the U.S., the total cost was over one billion dollars, nearly five times that of the 1970 census. The 1990 figure would of course be many times higher.

In the Indian context, there is no escape from census taking. So also, there is no escape from the escalating cost of the census. If National Sample Surveys are not free, why should the census enumeration be conducted almost free? According to the Census Commissioner,

"On an average, an enumerator had to canvass the schedules for about 600-750 people. A supervisor was appointed for every five enumerators. Reserve supervisors and enumerators were kept in readiness throughout the census operations. THe total number of enumerators and supervisors who carried out he 1991 Census was bout 1.7 million. Intensive training including practical training was imparted to this large number of field workers. A special form called "Post Graduate Degree Holders and Technical Personnel Schedule" was distributed to all the post graduates and technical degree holders on behalf of the Council for Scientific and Industrial Research to meet their needs for planning for technical and professional manpower. THe form was designed in the shape of the postage prepaid Inland letter to b filled by the respondent concerned. The enumerator was asked to collect it back, failing which the respondent was requested to mail it. The processing of this schedule and dissemination of the data will be the responsibility of the council for Scientific and Industrial Research.

Index

Acid rain, 102, 103
Air act 1981, 109
Air pollution, 101
Allelo chemistry, 181
Andrewartha and Birch, 67, 68
Annual world health, 202
Arms control and disarmament, agency, 8

Bhopal gas tragedy, 109
Biological Oxygen Demand (BOD), 99

Chipko movement, 113
Chemicals and pesticides use of, 92
Chloro-fluoro-carbons, 107
Consumption explosion, 6
Communicable diseases, 197
Committee on environment planning and coordination, 108
Critical stages of reproduction, 13

Dominance hierarchies, 140
Drosophila, 65

Environment, status of, 81
Environment, protection act, 109

Family size/nutritional status, 224
Family Planning Association of India, 16
Flora and Fauna, 91
Finland and Yugoslavia, 9
Fourth five year plan document, 108

Green house effect, 104

Health, indicators of, 187
Health definition, 185

International conference on population, 84
International planned parenthood federation, 84
International union of conservation of nature, 84

Lincoln index ration, 41, 42
Logistic theory of population, 62

Mahi, 99
Mammals and bacteria, 161
National seminar on population education, 16
National forest policy of 1952, 85

NATO and Warsaw Pact, 8
National Agriculture Commission, 11
National health programmes, 204
National health policy, 203
National nutrition programmes, 235
Nutrition and child survival, 221
Nutrition and fertility, 217
Nutritional deficiency diseases, 226
Ocean pollution, 100
Ozone depletion, 106

Population attributes, 38
Population cycles, 77
Population density, 44
Population debate, 2
Populations, ecology of, 37, 80
Population estimates, 41
Population education, definitions of, 19
Population education, historical perspectives, 13
Population education, need for, 10
Population education objectives of, 23
Population environment/resources, 81, 135
Population education, issues/trends in, 27
Population fluctuations, 70
Population and health, 185, 208
Population growth, trends in, 246
Population interaction, 149
Population regulation, social behaviour in, 141
Population, styles and development, 4
Population theories, 54

Random fluctuations, 72

Seasonal fluctuations, 70
Sex education, 17
Sex ratios and age structures, 48
Social behaviour, role of, 142
Sulphur dioxide, 101
Symbolic bacteria, 16
Symbiosis, 158
Sweden, 9

Teaching population dynamics, 13
Territorialism, 136
The population bomb, 3
Tragedy of the commons, 56

United Arab republic, 9
United nations declaration on population, 9
United States of America, 13
UNESCO's general conference, 14

Water Act 1974, 109
Water pollution, 97
World Commission on Environment and Development, 84
World Health Organisation, 7
World population, 1, 2
World plan of action, 15
World population growth, 97, 244
Workshop on population and family education, 15